Lecture Notes in Computer Science 12740

More information about this subseries at http://www.springer.com/series/7408

Frédéric Loulergue · Franz Wotawa (Eds.)

Tests and Proofs

15th International Conference, TAP 2021
Held as Part of STAF 2021
Virtual Event, June 21–22, 2021
Proceedings

 Springer

Editors
Frédéric Loulergue (iD)
Université d'Orléans
Orléans, France

Franz Wotawa (iD)
Graz University of Technology
Graz, Austria

ISSN 0302-9743   ISSN 1611-3349 (electronic)
Lecture Notes in Computer Science
ISBN 978-3-030-79378-4   ISBN 978-3-030-79379-1 (eBook)
https://doi.org/10.1007/978-3-030-79379-1

LNCS Sublibrary: SL2 – Programming and Software Engineering

This Springer imprint is published by the registered company Springer Nature Switzerland AG
The registered company address is: Gewerbestrasse 11, 6330 Cham, Switzerland

Preface

This volume contains the papers accepted for the 15th International Conference on Tests and Proofs (TAP 2021), originally planned to be held during June 21–22, 2021, in Bergen, Norway, as part of Software Technologies: Applications and Foundations (STAF), a federation of some of Europe's leading conferences on software technologies. Due to the COVID-19 pandemic, STAF and TAP were held online, and the TAP 2021 conference featured presentations of papers accepted at TAP 2020 and published in LNCS volume 12165, as well as the presentations of the papers published in this volume.

The TAP conference promotes research in verification and formal methods that targets the interplay of proofs and testing: the advancement of techniques of each kind and their combination, with the ultimate goal of improving software and system dependability.

Research in verification has seen a steady convergence of heterogeneous techniques and a synergy between the traditionally distinct areas of testing (and dynamic analysis) and of proving (and static analysis). Formal techniques for counter-example generation based on, for example, symbolic execution, SAT/SMT-solving or model checking, furnish evidence for the potential of a combination of test and proof. The combination of predicate abstraction with testing-like techniques based on exhaustive enumeration opens the perspective for novel techniques of proving correctness. On the practical side, testing offers cost-effective debugging techniques of specifications or crucial parts of program proofs (such as invariants). Last but not least, testing is indispensable when it comes to the validation of the underlying assumptions of complex system models involving hardware or system environments. Over the years, there is growing acceptance in research communities that testing and proving are complementary rather than mutually exclusive techniques.

TAP 2021 received 13 abstracts that led to 10 submissions out of which we accepted 6 papers after review and discussion with the Program Committee (PC) members. The submissions came from authors in the following countries (in alphabetical order): France, Germany, India, Japan, New Zealand, Russia, Singapore, Sweden, the UK, and the USA. We thank the PC members and reviewers for doing an excellent job!

For the third time, TAP featured an artifact evaluation (AE) and three papers were awarded with AE badges. We thank the AE chairs, Daniel Dietsch (University of Freiburg, Germany) and Marie-Christine Jakobs (TU Darmstadt, Germany), for organizing artifact submission and evaluation, and the AE Committee members for thoroughly evaluating all artifacts.

This volume also contains two short abstracts: an abstract of the talk given by our invited speaker, Mohammad Mousavi (University of Leicester, UK), on "Learning About the Change: An Adaptive Approach to Automata Learning", and an abstract of our invited tutorial on Runtime Verification led by Martin Leucker (University of Lübeck, Germany).

We thank the organizing team of STAF in Bergen, in particular Adrian Rutle who had to deal with a very difficult situation. We also thank the publication team at Springer for their support. We hope that you will enjoy reading the volume.

May 2021
Frédéric Loulergue
Franz Wotawa

Organization

Program Committee Chairs

Frédéric Loulergue   Université d'Orléans, France
Franz Wotawa   Graz University of Technology, Austria

Program Committee

Wolfgang Ahrendt   Chalmers University of Technology, Sweden
Bernhard K. Aichernig   TU Graz, Austria
Dirk Beyer   LMU Munich, Germany
Achim D. Brucker   University of Exeter, UK
Simon Cruanes   Imandra, USA
Catherine Dubois   ENSIIE, France
Cédric Eichler   INSA Centre Val de Loire, France
Gordon Fraser   University of Passau, Germany
Alex Groce   Northern Arizona University, USA
Klaus Havelund   Jet Propulsion Laboratory, USA
Chantal Keller   Université Paris-Sud, France
Nikolai Kosmatov   CEA List, France
Martin Leucker   University of Lübeck, Germany
Karl Meinke   KTH Royal Institute of Technology, Sweden
Stephan Merz   Inria, France
Corina Pasareanu   NASA, USA
François Pessaux   ENSTA Paris, France
Ingo Pill   Silicon Austria Labs, Austria
Heike Wehrheim   University of Paderborn, Germany
Burkhart Wolff   Université Paris-Sud, France
Nina Yevtushenko   Ivannikov Institute for System Programming of RAS, Russia

Artifact Evaluation Committee Chairs

Marie-Christine Jakobs   TU Darmstadt, Germany
Danie Dietsch   University of Freiburg, Germany

Artifact Evaluation Committee

Patrice Clemente   INSA Centre Val de Loire, France
Simon Dierl   TU Dortmund, Germany
Mathias Fleury   Johannes Kepler University Linz, Austria
Michael Foster   University of Sheffield, UK

Ákos Hajdu	Budapest University of Technology and Economics, Hungary
Jan Haltermann	Paderborn University, Germany
Marcel Hark	RWTH Aachen University, Germany
Sean Kauffman	Aalborg University, Denmark
Sven Linker	Lancaster University (Leipzig), Germany
Cyrus Liu	Stevens Institute of Technology, USA
Marco Muniz	Aalborg University, Denmark
Yakoub Nemouchi	University of York, UK
Virgile Robles	CEA List, France
Martin Sachenbacher	University of Lübeck, Germany
Christian Schilling	University of Konstanz, Germany
Martin Tappler	Graz University of Technology, Austria
Nico Weise	Ludwig-Maximilians-Universität München, Germany

Steering Committee

Bernhardt K. Aichernig	TU Graz, Austria
Jasmin Blanchette	Vrije Universiteit Amsterdam, Netherlands
Achim D. Brucker	University of Sheffield, UK
Catherine Dubois (Chair)	ENSIIE, France
Martin Gogolla	University of Bremen, Germany
Nikolai Kosmatov	CEA, France
Burkhart Wolff	LRI, France

Additional Reviewers

Eduard Kamburjan
Karam Kharraz
Ashfaq Hussain Farooqui
Delphine Longuet

Abstracts of Invited Events

Learning About the Change: An Adaptive Approach to Automata Learning

Mohammad Reza Mousavi

University of Leicester, UK

Automata learning is a technique to learn behavioural models from black-box systems. Variability and evolution are inherent to much of the modern autonomous systems and hence, new sorts of automata learning techniques are needed to learn about variability-intensive and evolving systems. In this talk, we first present the basic principles of automata learning and then report on two novel techniques for learning variability-annotated models as well as efficient learning for evolving systems by identifying the commonalities and differences in the learning process.

This talk is based on joint work with several people, and in particular, with Diego Damasceno and Adenilso Simao.

Testing, Runtime Verification and Automata Learning

Martin Leucker

University of Lübeck, Germany

Testing and runtime verification are both verification techniques for checking whether a system is correct. The essential artefacts for checking whether the system is correct are actual executions of the system, formally words. Such a set of words should be representative for the systems behavior.

In the field of automata learning (or grammatical inference) a formal model of a system is derived based on exemplifying behavior. In other words, the question is addressed what model fits to a given set of words.

In testing, typically, the system under test is examined on a finite set of test cases, formally words, which may be derived manually or automatically. Oracle-based testing is a form of testing in which an oracle, typically a manually developed piece of code, is attached to the system under test and employed for checking whether a given set of test cases passes or fails.

In runtime verification, typically, a formal specification of the correct behavior is given from which a so-called monitor is synthesised and used for examining whether the behavior of the system under test, or generally the system to monitor, adheres to such a specification. In a sense, the monitor acts as a test oracle, when employed in testing.

From the discussion above we see that testing, runtime verification, and learning automata share similarities but also differences. The main artefacts used for the different methods are formal specifications, models like automata, but especially sets of words, on which the different system descriptions are compared, to eventually obtain a verdict whether the system under test is correct or not.

In this tutorial we recall the basic ideas of testing, oracle-based testing, model-based testing, conformance testing, automata learning and runtime verification and elaborate on a coherent picture with the above mentioned artefacts as ingredients. We mostly refrain from technical details but concentrate on the big picture of those verification techniques.

Contents

Learning, Test Resource Allocation
and Benchmarks

Use Case Testing: A Constrained Active Machine Learning Approach

Karl Meinke$^{(\boxtimes)}$ and Hojat Khosrowjerdi

School of Electrical Engineering and Computer Science,
KTH Royal Institute of Technology, 100 44 Stockholm, Sweden
karlm@kth.se

Abstract. As a methodology for system design and testing, use cases are well-known and widely used. While current active machine learning (ML) algorithms can effectively automate unit testing, they do not scale up to use case testing of complex systems in an efficient way.

We present a new parallel distributed processing (PDP) architecture for a constrained active machine learning (CAML) approach to use case testing. To exploit CAML we introduce a use case modeling language with: (i) compile-time constraints on query generation, and (ii) run-time constraints using dynamic constraint checking. We evaluate this approach by applying a prototype implementation of CAML to use case testing of simulated multi-vehicle autonomous driving scenarios.

Keywords: Autonomous driving · Constraint solving · Learning-based testing · Machine learning · Model checking · Requirements testing · Use case testing

1 Introduction

For the design and testing of complex software systems, the use case approach has a long history emerging from [20] with many proposed variations and refinements. A use case can be viewed as a recurring short story in the daily life of a system. The essence of use case driven software engineering (SE) is to focus on a limited number of commonly occurring scenarios whose correct design and reliable implementation can generate significant end user benefit. For example, for cyber-physical systems, a focus on recurrent high-risk use cases can benefit end user safety.

By modeling system interactions with external actors, use cases open the way to evaluating a system in different environments and scenarios. In general, there can be a vast number of potential contexts so parameter modeling can be crucial. An environment is discretised into agents known as actors, which can be humans or other software systems. Through modeling short dialogs between system and environment within constrained scenarios, use cases capture important context sensitive behavioural information that can be used to test system implementations.

F. Loulergue and F. Wotawa (Eds.): TAP 2021, LNCS 12740, pp. 3–21, 2021.
https://doi.org/10.1007/978-3-030-79379-1_1

The development of UML languages, such as sequence diagrams, has made it possible to bridge the gap between informal natural language models of use cases and precise machine readable formats suitable for automated test case generation (TCG). Consequently, there is a significant literature on TCG for use cases from UML models surveyed in [32].

However, for automated TCG, machine learning (ML) based approaches such as black-box checking [30] and learning-based testing [26] are also worthy of consideration. For unit testing, such methods have been shown to be both effective [10,18,22,23] and efficient [35] for finding errors in real-world systems. For use case testing, active ML offers the possibility to systematically and efficiently explore the variability inherent in different *use case parameters* as well as the *time dimension*. Furthermore, by reverse engineering a model of the system under test (SUT), ML can be easily combined with static analysis techniques such as model checking and constraint solving. Unfortunately, current active ML algorithms in the literature provide no support for use case constraints and therefore scale rather poorly to use case testing.

In this paper, we propose a new and more scalable ML-based testing approach suitable for use case testing. This approach is termed *constrained active machine learning* (CAML). It generalises the ML techniques for dynamic software analysis surveyed in [3] by inferring *chains of intersecting automaton models*. Our proposal combines three new techniques that improve scalability: (i) a parallel distributed processing (PDP) architecture that supports concurrent test execution, (ii) use case modeling constructs that sequence and constrain ML parameters at compile time, and (iii) use case modeling constructs that constrain and dynamically bound ML parameters at runtime (the training phase). While these new techniques can undoubtedly be extended and optimised for even better scalability, we will show that they suffice to tackle non-trivial testing problems such as advanced driver assistance systems (ADAS) in multi-vehicle use case scenarios.

The structure of the paper is as follows. In Sect. 2, we discuss the background, including scalability problems for current active ML algorithms. In Sect. 3, we describe the architecture of a constrained active ML approach to testing. In Sect. 4, we present a use case modeling language that makes available the capabilities of the CAML architecture. In Sect. 5, we present a systematic evaluation and benchmarking of a prototype implementation of CAML. We have integrated a CAML prototype with the commercial vehicle simulation tool ASM produced by dSPACE GmbH[1]. The resulting toolchain allows us to model and test four industry-standard use cases for an *adaptive cruise controller* (ACC) in multi-vehicle scenarios ranging from 2 to 4 vehicles. In Sect. 6, we discuss the results of this evaluation. In Sect. 7, we survey related approaches. Finally, in Sect. 8, we discuss conclusions and possible future extensions of our approach.

---

[1] See www.dspace.com.

2 Background and Problem Statement

2.1 Use Case Modeling

A use case describes a system in terms of its interaction with the world. In the popular account [13], a use case consists of a *main success scenario* which is a numbered list of steps, and optionally one or more *extension scenarios* which are also numbered lists. A *step* is an event or action of the system itself or of an interacting agent known as an *actor*. Structurally, main and extension scenarios are the same, i.e. an enumeration of actions describing an interaction between the system and external actors. The difference is simply interpretation: extensions are "a condition that results in different interactions from ... the main success scenario" [13]. The template approach to use cases of [8] is more expressive. It includes both preconditions and success guarantees. We model these two concepts as constraints in our approach, as they are relevant for both efficient TCG and test verdict construction. The sequence diagram language of UML [9] generalises these linear sequences of actions to allow branches, loops and concurrency. The live sequence chart (LSC) language of [16] goes even further than UML by integrating temporal logic concepts and modalities (so called hot and cold conditions). Our approach could be extended to cover these advanced features, but they are not the subject of this initial research. Nevertheless, we will borrow simple temporal logic constructs to constrain TCG using ML.

2.2 Active Automaton Learning

By active automaton learning (see e.g. [17,21]) we mean the use of heuristic algorithms to dynamically generate new queries and acquire training data online during the training phase[2]. This contrasts with passive learning, where an a priori fixed training set is used. Since pioneering results of [1,14], it has been known that active ML has the capability to speed up the training process compared with passive ML. Recently, active automaton learning algorithms such as Angluin's L* [1] have experienced renewed interest from the software engineering community. Active automaton learning can be applied to learn behavioural models of black-box software systems. Such models can be used for SE needs such as code analysis, testing and documentation. A recent survey of active ML for SE is [2].

In automaton learning, the task is to infer the behavior of an unknown black-box system, aka. the *system under learning* (SUL), as an automaton model, e.g. a finite state Moore machine[3] $A = (\Sigma, \Omega, S, s_0, \delta : \Sigma \times S \to S, \lambda : S \to \Omega)$. This model is constructed from a finite set of observations of the input/output

---

[2] Since the new training data is generated by heuristic algorithms alone, active ML is *not* the same as interactive ML which requires human intervention.

[3] Here Σ is a finite input alphabet, Ω is a finite or infinite output alphabet, S is a finite state set, $s_0 \in S$ is the initial state, δ is the state transition function and λ is the output function. δ is extended to a transition function on input sequences $\delta^* : \Sigma^* \times S \to S$ by iteration.

behaviour of the SUL. During the training phase, a single step consists of heuristically generating a finite input sequence $\bar{i} = (i_1, ..., i_n) \in \Sigma^*$ as a query about the SUL. This query $\bar{i}$ must be answered by the SUL online with a response $\bar{o} = (o_1, ..., o_n) \in \Omega^*$. By iterating this single step, the learning algorithm compiles a growing list of queries $\bar{i}_1, ..., \bar{i}_k$ and their responses, $\bar{o}_1, ..., \bar{o}_k$ for increasing $k = 1, 2, ...$ This is the training data for A. As the training data grows, increasingly accurate models[4] $A_i : i = 0, 1, ...$ of the SUL can be constructed[5]. Different active learning algorithms generate different query sets. For example, the L* algorithm [1] maintains an expanding 2-dimensional table of queries and responses, where new gaps in the table represent new active queries.

Note that each new hypothesis model A_i must be checked for behavioral equivalence with the SUL to terminate learning. Equivalence checking is a second source of active queries and there are well known algorithms for this e.g. [34]. Probabilistic equivalence checking, by random sampling, is a common blackbox method and the basis for *probably approximately correct* (PAC) automaton learning [21].

Equivalence checking avoids the problem of premature termination of the training phase with an incomplete model. Thus, many active learning algorithms such as L* can be proved convergent and terminating in polynomial time under general conditions. This means that under reasonable assumptions about queries and the structure of the SUL, eventually some hypothesis A_i will be behaviourally equivalent to the SUL.

2.3   Problem Statement: Scalable ML

Active machine learning can be used to automate the software testing process, a technique known as *black-box checking* (BBC) [30] or more generally *learning-based testing* (LBT) [26]. These approaches leverage active query generation as a source of test cases, and the SUL role is played by the software *system under test* (SUT). They are very effective for unit testing (see e.g. [10,18,22,23]) where the set of possible SUT inputs, and their temporal order, are very loosely constrained, if at all. They can achieve high test coverage and outperform other techniques such as randomised testing [35]. The BBC/LBT approaches both arise as a special case of our more general use case approach (c.f. Sect. 3.2), namely as a *single step use case* with the constant gate predicate `false`.

In contrast to unit testing, use case testing evaluates focused, temporally ordered and goal directed dialogues between the system and its environment (see e.g. [12]). Here, a test *fail* implies some non-conformity between the SUT and an intended use case model. Active machine learning can potentially automate use case testing, with the obvious advantages of test automation (speed, reliability, high coverage).

---

[4] The A_i grow in size during active learning. The relationship between k and i varies between learning algorithms.

[5] A unified algebraic view of different automaton construction methods is the quotient automaton construction. Further details can be found in [3].

However, in the context of use case testing, two assumptions used in current active automata learning algorithms (such as L*) fail. *Assumption 1:* every input value $i \in \Sigma$ is possible for every use case step. *Problem 1:* This assumption leads to a large number of irrelevant test cases since test values are applied out of context (i.e. relevant use case step). *Assumption 2:* Every sequential combination of input values $(i_1, ..., i_n) \in \Sigma^*$ is a valid use case test. *Problem 2:* This assumption also leads to a large number of irrelevant test cases since most sequential combinations of test values will not fulfill the final or even the intermediate goals of the use case.

The combination of test redundancy arising from Problems 1 and 2 leads to an exponentially growing test suite (in the length of the use case) with very many irrelevant and/or redundant test cases.

Problem Statement: *The key problem to be solved for applying active ML to use case testing is to constrain the training phase, so that a scalable set of scenario-relevant test cases is generated.*

We decompose our solution to this problem by solving Problem 1 using static (compile-time) constraints, and solving Problem 2 using dynamic (run-time or training) constraints. Our approach is an instance of applying ML for its *generative aspect* [11], i.e. the capability to generate and explore solutions to constraints by machine learning.

3   Constrained Active Machine Learning (CAML)

In this section, we introduce a generic architecture for use case testing by CAML. This architecture aims to overcome the scalability problems of active ML identified in Sect. 2.3.

3.1   Use Case Testing: An Example

We can motivate our CAML architecture from the modeling needs of a well-known embedded software application from the automotive sector.

An *adaptive cruise controller* (ACC) is an example of a modern ADAS application used as a component for semi- and fully autonomous driving. An ACC is a control algorithm designed to regulate the longitudinal distance between two vehicles. The context for use is that a host vehicle H (that deploys the ACC) is following behind a leader vehicle L. When the ACC is engaged, it automatically maintains a chosen safety gap (measured in time or distance) between H and L. Typically, a radar on H senses the distance to L, and the ACC monitors and maintains the inter-vehicle gap smoothly by gas and brake actions on H. An important use case for testing ACC implementations[6] is known as *cut-in-and-brake* (C&B). The C&B use case consists of four steps.

---

[6] Many ACC algorithms exist in the literature, see e.g. [37].

Step 1: Initially H is following L (actor 1) along one lane of a road. Along an adjacent lane, an overtaking vehicle O (actor 2) approaches H from behind and overtakes.

Step 2: After O achieves some longitudinal distance d ahead of H, O changes lanes to enter the gap between H and L.

Step 3: When O has finished changing lane, it brakes for some short time.

Step 4: O releases its brake and resumes travel.

The C&B use case is clearly hazardous for both H and O, with highest collision risk during Steps 2 and 3. Safety critical parameters such as d above may be explicit or implicit in a use case description, and their boundary values are often unknown. These may need to be identified by testing [4]. Active ML is a powerful technology for such parameter exploration.

Extensive testing of use cases such as C&B is routinely carried out in the automotive industry. A *test case* for C&B consists of a *time series* of parameter values for vehicle actuators such as gas, brake and steering, to control the trajectories of H, O and L. The lengths of each individual Step 1–4 are not explicitly stated by the use case definition above. These constitute additional test parameters. Chosen parameter values must satisfy the constraints of Steps 1–4 to make a valid C&B scenario. Notice that H is longitudinally autonomous as long as the ACC is engaged, and can be fully autonomous on straight road sections. So only the trajectory parameters of L and O can be directly controlled in this case. Clearly random testing, i.e. randomised choice of test parameter values, is not useful here. Most random trajectories for L and O do not satisfy the criteria for C&B, and would represent extremely haphazard driving, uncharacteristic of real life. For a given use case U, valid test cases are *constrained time series*, and we must address efficient constraint satisfaction in any practical ML solution.

3.2   A Parallel Distributed CAML Architecture

Following the connectionist or parallel distributed processing (PDP) paradigm, we introduce a pipeline architecture for CAML in Fig. 1. This architecture consists of a linear pipeline of alternate *active automaton learning modules* L_i and *model checking modules* MC_i. Each learner L_i conducts online active ML on a *cloned copy* SUT_i of the SUT.

For use case testing, the basic idea is to dedicate each learning algorithm L_i to the task of learning Step i, for all the $i = 1, ..., n$ steps of an n-step use case U. We will show later, in Sect. 4, how the use case U is modeled by constraints. Here we focus on explaining and motivating the PDP architecture of Fig. 1.

Each learner L_i has the task to infer an automaton model A_i of Step i in U by actively generating queries[7] $in_\alpha = in_{\alpha,1}, ..., in_{\alpha,l(\alpha)} \in \Sigma_i^*$ and executing them on SUT_i. We may refer to A_i as the *state space model* for Step i. Constraining the input for SUT_i to the input alphabet Σ_i in Step i at compile time significantly reduces the search space for finding valid use case tests for U as whole. This

---

[7] The queries have variable length $l(\alpha)$.

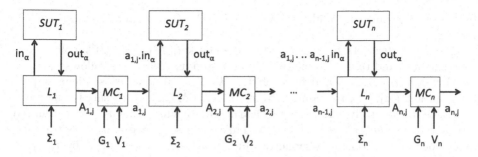

Fig. 1. A constrained active ML architecture

addresses Problem 1 of Sect. 2.3. Each query in_α is executed locally on SUT_i. The observed output behaviour $out_\alpha = out_{\alpha,1}, ..., out_{\alpha,l(\alpha)} \in \Omega_i^*$ of SUT_i is integrated by L_i into the current version $A_{i,j}$ of A_i to incrementally generate a sequence of approximations $A_{i,1}, A_{i,2}, ...$ that converge to A_i, as described in Sect. 2.2.

We can observe in the use case C&B that the end of each Step i is characterised by a Boolean condition G_i that must become *true* to enter the next Step $i + 1$ or else to finish the use case. For example: we leave Step 1 of C&B and start Step 2, once the gap between O and H exceeds d and not before. To constrain and connect each adjacent pair of state space models A_i and A_{i+1}, constructed independently by L_i and L_{i+1}, we model G_i as a Boolean constraint $G_i \subseteq \Omega_i$ which is a *predicate* on state values $\lambda(s) \in \Omega_i$. We term G_i the *gate condition* for Step i. The gate condition G_i can be seen as both the *success guarantee* for leaving Step i and the *precondition* for entering Step $i + 1$ (c.f. Sect. 2.1). In particular, G_n is a success guarantee for finishing the entire use case U.

Figure 1 shows a second Boolean constraint or predicate $V_i \subseteq \Omega_i$ called the *verdict condition*. This will be discussed later in Sect. 4.3.

The gate condition G_i is evaluated on each approximation $A_{i,j}$ of A_i, for $j = 1, 2, ...$ by the model checker MC_i (c.f. Fig. 1). Model checking [7] is a general constraint solving technique for Boolean and temporal logic formulas on automaton models. The model checker MC_i incrementally analyses each $A_{i,j}$ to identify a new state $s_{i,j} \in S_{i,j}$ for $A_{i,j}$ (not previously seen in $A_{i,j-1}$) that satisfies the gate G_i, i.e. G_i is *true* as a predicate on $\lambda(s_{i,j})$. The state $s_{i,j}$ will become an initial state of A_{i+1}. In this way, adjacent models A_i and A_{i+1} intersect, and $A_1, ..., A_n$ collectively build a complete and connected chain of automaton models of U.

Now, a guaranteed condition of automaton learning algorithms such as L* is that every learned state $s \in S_{i,j}$ is *reachable* in $A_{i,j}$ by at least one *access sequence* $a = a_1, ..., a_m \in \Sigma_i^*$, i.e. $\delta_i^*(a, s_0) = s$. The model checker MC_i can return such an access sequence $a_{i,j}$ for state $s_{i,j}$ satisfying gate G_i. This access sequence $a_{i,j}$ is a valid *test case solution* for Step i of U and hence a *partial solution* to a complete and valid test case for U. Dynamic constraint solving using MC_i at runtime further constrains the size of the state space to be searched in building valid test cases for U. This approach addresses Problem 2 of Sect. 2.3.

The active learners $L_1, ..., L_n$ and model checkers $MC_1, ..., MC_n$ collaborate to construct valid test cases for the whole n-step use case U as follows.

For each $j = 1, 2, ...$ and for each $1 \leq k < n$, all k access sequences (partial solutions) $a_{1,j}, ..., a_{k,j}$ coming from $MC_1, ..., MC_k$ (which satisfy the gates $G_1, ..., G_k$ respectively) are passed to learner L_{k+1} where they are concatenated into a *setup sequence*[8] $(a_{1,j}, \ldots, a_{k,j})$. This setup sequence is used as a prefix, and appended in front of every active query $in_\alpha \in \Sigma_{k+1}^*$ generated by L_{k+1}. A complete active query for SUT_{k+1} therefore has the form:

$$(a_{1,j}, \ldots, a_{k,j}, in_\alpha).$$

From the corresponding output sequence $out_\alpha \in \Omega_{k+1}^*$ returned by SUT_{k+1} only the final suffix of length $|in_\alpha|$ is retained by L_{k+1} to construct A_{k+1}. This suppresses all SUT output due to the setup sequence $a_{1,j} . \ldots . a_{k,j}$. So the state space model A_{k+1} only contains information about Step $k+1$ of U, and we avoid duplication of effort between the parallel learners.

Finally the n access sequences (partial solutions), which emerge periodically from $MC_1, ..., MC_n$, are concatenated to form

$$a_j = (a_{1,j}, \ldots, a_{n,j}).$$

Thus a_j represents the j-th complete test case for U, as a concatenation of the j-th partial solutions. The test case a_j satisfies all of the guards $G_1, ..., G_n$, in particular the final goal G_n of U. Moreover, in each of the steps $a_{i,j}$ all actions are constrained to Σ_i^*. So a_j is a valid test case for U.

4   A Use Case Modeling Language for CAML

We can now introduce a constraint-based modeling language for use cases that exploits the CAML architecture of Sect. 3.2. A constraint model U will capture an informal use case description in terms of parameters and constraints suitable for using in the CAML architecture. These include: Σ_i, G_i and V_i for each step $i = 1, ..., n$.

4.1   Input/Output Declaration

Recall the running example of the C&B use case from Sect. 3.1. The actors are the three vehicles H (with its ACC), L and O. The first modeling step is to decide what actor parameters we need to control and observe. Much automotive application testing is performed within the safety of a virtual environment such as a multi-vehicle simulator. Whatever the context, we can assume the existence

---

[8] This terminology comes from testing theory and is used to denote an initialisation sequence bringing SUT_{k+1} into a state where in_α can be applied.

of a test harness or wrapper around the SUT which exposes the SUT API in a standardised and symbolic way, as a set of variable names and their types: float, integer, enumeration, Boolean, etc.

This modeling activity for C&B identifies the following minimum sets[9] of relevant input and output parameters and their types:

```
input_variables = [SpeedL:enum, SpeedO:enum, SteerO:enum];
```

This statement declares three test input variables (from the SUT API) of enumeration type enum that will control the leader vehicle speed, the overtaker speed and the overtaker steering[10]. So a *test input vector* to the SUT is an ordered triple of enum values (x_1, x_2, x_3). A complete *use case test input* is a finite sequence of test input vectors (c.f. Fig. 2(a)) ((x_1^1, x_2^1, x_3^1), ..., (x_1^n, x_2^n, x_3^n)).

For the output variables, the model declaration is:

```
output_variables = [Crash:boolean, O2HDist:float, TimeDev:float];
```

This statement declares three test output variables (from the SUT API) for crash detection, O-to-H longitudinal distance and time gap deviation (as a percentage error) between the intended ACC time gap[11] (H-to-L) and the observed time gap (H-to-L). A *test output vector* from the SUT is an ordered triple of values (y_1, y_2, y_3), where y_1 ranges over Boolean and y_2 and y_3 over float values. A *use case test output* is a finite sequence of test output vectors (c.f. Fig. 2(b)) ((y_1^1, y_2^1, y_3^1), ..., (y_1^n, y_2^n, y_3^n)).

4.2   Sequencing, Static and Dynamic Constraints

Next we declare the four steps of the C&B use case in terms of: (i) compile time constraints on the input alphabets Σ_i and (ii) runtime constraints on the gate predicates G_i.

```
input_values[1] = { 50,55:SpeedL, 55,60,65:SpeedO, 0:SteerO };
gate[1] = when( O2HDist >= 5.0 & O2HDist <= 40.0 );
input_values[2] = { 50:SpeedL, right_100_4:SteerO, 50:SpeedO };
gate[2] = when( time >= 4.0 );
input_values[3] = { 60:SpeedL, 25,30,35:SpeedO, 0:SteerO };
gate[3] = when( TimeDev <= 5.0 );
input_values[4] = { 50:SpeedL, 60:SpeedO, 0:SteerO };
gate[4] = when( time >= 5.0 );
```

Each declaration input_values[i] symbolically declares Σ_i, the input values for Step i in the notation of Sect. 3.2. In general, values for Σ_i are sampled within

---

[9] Our example is pedagogic only. A more realistic model for C&B has more parameters and values.

[10] Recall that H is autonomous, hence only L and O are controllable in this scenario.

[11] The intended time gap is here assumed to be a fixed nominal value for every test case, typically around 1.5–2.5 s. It is often assignable by the driver of H.

the typical range of values (e.g. vehicle speeds) characteristic for each step of the use case (e.g. an acceleration, steady or deceleration step). For example, in Step 1 above, variable SpeedL has possible values 50,55, SpeedO has possible values 55,60,65 but SteerO takes only the value 0. The steering value 0 is a neutral command (i.e. straight ahead) in Steps 1, 3 and 4. However in Step 2 (the lane change step for overtaker O), the steering value right_100_4 generates a sigmoidal right curve for O across 100% of the lane width in 4 time steps[12]. Notice that the declared speed of O drops from 50 in Step 2 to 25, 30 or 35 in Step 3. This implements the braking action of O in Step 3 (which need not even be a constant deceleration).

The informal meaning of gate[i] = when(state_predicate); is that once SUT execution has entered Step i, it stays in this step until a state is encountered that satisfies state_predicate. At this point SUT execution may pass to the next Step $i + 1$. Thus gate[1] = when(O2HDist >= 5.0 & O2HDist <= 40.0); captures the transition from overtaking in Step 1 to lane change in Step 2 by setting specific minimum and maximum boundary values for d of 5.0 and 40.0 metres (c.f. the C&B description of Sect. 3.1). A gate condition can also take account of time, for example gate[2] = when(time >= 4.0); ensures that we maintain the steering command of Step 2 for 4 time steps, relative to the start of Step 2. This ensures the steering action is completed.

The formalised C&B model above illustrates some of the variety of CAML capabilities for modeling a single step of a use case. These capabilities range from a single action that must be performed exactly once (Step 2 above) to a set of possible actions that can be executed in non-deterministic order over a time interval that is either: (i) unspecified, (ii) constant, (iii) finite and bounded or (iv) unbounded. Steps 1, 3 and 4 above illustrate some of these options. Each single step activity is defined by a judicious combination of input alphabets, gate constraints and step ordering. We have not attempted to be exhaustive in modeling all possible single step capabilities, and further extensions are possible (see Sect. 8).

4.3   Automated Test Verdict Construction

Recalling the discussion of Sect. 3.1, we can say informally that a (4 step) use case test input $a_j = a_{1,j} \ldots a_{4,j}$ for C&B has a *pass* verdict if none of the vehicles O, L or H collide. Otherwise a_j has a *fail* verdict. The model checkers MC_i automate *test verdict construction* for each use case test input a_j as follows.

A use case test input $a_j = (a_{1,j} \ldots a_{n,j})$ for an n-step use case U has the verdict *pass* if, and only if $v_{i,j} = pass$ for each $i = 1, ..., n$, where $v_{i,j} \in \{pass, fail\}$ is the *local verdict* for the test case step $a_{i,j}$ (which is an access sequence). Each model checker MC_i is used to evaluate its local verdict $v_{i,j}$ on $a_{i,j}$ in a distributed manner. In general, $v_{i,j}$ is based on a specific local criterion $V_i \subseteq \Omega_i$ for Step i as a predicate or constraint on state values $\lambda(s)$ for $s \in S_i$ a

---

[12] The time step length is also a fixed nominal value for all test cases.

state in the automaton model A_i. Figure 1 shows how the verdict predicates V_i are integrated into the CAML architecture. For C&B we are mainly interested in vehicle crashes in Steps 2 and 3 as the most hazardous steps. We can therefore extend the use case model of Sect. 4.2 with local verdict constraints for Steps 2 and 3 as follows:

```
verdict[2] = always( !crash );
verdict[3] = always( !crash & TimeDev <= 50.0);
```

The informal meaning of `verdict[i] = always( state_predicate );` is that `state_predicate` should remain *true* throughout Step i and if it becomes false at any point during Step i then both Step i, and the whole test case fail. For example, in `verdict[3]` for Step 3 above, when O is braking, we add to the no-crash requirement the additional verdict requirement that the observed time gap deviation `TimeDev` does not exceed 50%. This increases the safety margin of the ACC.

For the i-th access sequence $a_{i,j} = a_{i,j,1}, ..., a_{i,j,m} \in \Sigma_i^*$ of a_j, the model checker MC_i evaluates the verdict predicate V_i on $\lambda(s_{i,j,k})$ for each of the corresponding states $s_{i,j,1}, ..., s_{i,j,m} \in S_{i,j}$ traversed by $a_{i,j}$ in $A_{i,j}$. Here $s_{i,j,1}$ is the initial state of $A_{i,j}$ and $s_{i,j,m}$ is the final state that satisfies the gate condition G_i. If $\lambda(s_{i,j,k})$ satisfies V_i for each $k = 1, ..., m$ then $v_{i,j} = pass$ otherwise $v_{i,j} = fail$.

5   Evaluation and Benchmarking

To evaluate our CAML architecture for machine learning and its associated use case modeling language, we implemented these in a prototype TCG tool. This prototype was then integrated with the commercial vehicle software simulator ASM to provide a complete toolchain for testing driving scenarios in a virtualised road environment.

We conducted an evaluation of the complete toolchain to benchmark the speed and effectiveness of the CAML approach. For evaluation purposes, we chose use cases for an ACC-equipped semi-autonomous vehicle driven in multi-vehicle scenarios.

5.1   ROBOTest: A CAML Implementation

We implemented a prototype of the CAML architecture of Sect. 3, termed ROBOTest, on top of the ML-based testing tool LBTest [27]. LBTest has previously been successfully used in unit testing of automotive ECU software [22,23], as well as other domains including web and finance [36]. LBTest supports important features necessary for realistic testing case studies, such as infinite and continuous test parameter types (including integers, strings, floating point numbers), multi-threaded learning for high data throughput, and configuration files for job specification and test session management. In particular, a ROBOTest use case model of the type presented in Sect. 4 is simply added to an LBTest configuration file. During a testing session, multiple instances of LBTest `Learner` and `ModelChecker` classes implement the PDP architecture of Sect. 3.2.

Table 1. ML-based testing results for four ADAS use cases

No.	Use case	Use case steps	Use case vehicles	Ego vehicle autonomy	Executed test cases	Total execution time	Errors found	Learned model size
1	Following lead	2	2	Full	227	1 h 0 min 10 s	No	140 states
2	Cut-in	4	3	Full	761	20 min 29 s	Yes	177 states
3	Cut-out	4	3	Full	36	2 min 50 s	No	122 states
4	Overtake	5	4	Semi	1654	5 h 21 min 15 s	Yes	1022 states

5.2   Integration of ROBOTest and ASM

The ASM vehicle simulator from dSPACE GmbH provides the capability to perform software in the loop (SiL) testing of automotive applications. It can be used to produce realistic simulations of automotive applications in multi-vehicle scenarios. The ego vehicle parameters, road and environment parameters and the numbers and types of traffic objects are all configured before a simulation starts. The basic approach to ROBOTest and ASM tool integration was to expose key attributes of a parameterised ASM traffic model through a lightweight wrapper. By communicating indirectly with ASM through the wrapper, ego vehicle and traffic object commands could be accessed from the ROBOTest use case model contained in a configuration file. Such commands include parameterized commands to the ego vehicle and traffic objects for steering, gas, brake etc. Several command examples can be seen in the C&B use case of Sect. 4.

The wrapper was delegated the responsibility to translate ML generated use case tests into timed sequences of vehicle commands, and dispatch these sequences to the simulator. Key simulator variables were then logged by ASM and recovered by the wrapper. The resulting observation sequences were returned to ROBOTest for learning.

As the target language for test case translation, we used the ASM scenario language to specify the detailed actions of the ego vehicle and traffic objects. This was done in the scenario editor of the ASM ModelDesk application. ModelDesk also takes care of the road environment definitions and downloading configuration parameters into the ASM VEOS platform.

5.3   ACC Use Case Descriptions

To evaluate the toolchain resulting from integrating the two tools ROBOTest and ASM, we chose a set of use cases for an ACC application bundled with the ASM license. The choice was guided by the need for different use case lengths, complexity and number of actors. The following four use cases for an ACC-equipped ego vehicle in a multi-vehicle traffic environment were chosen.

1. Following Lead. The ego-vehicle follows a lead vehicle in the same lane, i.e. it is tracking the lead as its target. The lead vehicle accelerates and decelerates within given speed bounds. The ego vehicle should adapt its speed and maintain its predefined time-gap.

2. Cut-in (c.f. Sect. 4). The ego-vehicle follows a lead vehicle (aka. leader1) in the same lane that has a constant speed. A cut-in vehicle (aka. leader2) drives behind the ego vehicle in an adjacent lane. The cut-in vehicle overtakes the ego vehicle and then performs a cut-in maneuver with constant speed, while leader1 maintains its constant speed. The cut-in vehicle should be selected as target when it has crossed the lane marking. The ego vehicle ACC should re-establish the intended time gap with cut-in as the new lead vehicle (leader2).

3. Cut-out. The ego-vehicle follows a cut-out vehicle in the same lane with constant speed. The cut-out vehicle (aka. leader1) follows another vehicle leader2 in the same lane. The cut-out vehicle speed is not faster than leader2. The cut-out vehicle changes to an adjacent lane and speeds up to overtake leader2. The ego vehicle ACC should re-establish the time gap to leader2 as the new target vehicle to be followed.

4. Overtake. The ego-vehicle follows a lead vehicle leader1 in the same lane. The ego vehicle performs a manual lane change to the adjacent lane, and then speeds up to overtake leader1. Another vehicle leader2 is already driving ahead in the adjacent lane and lies front of the ego vehicle after its lane change. The ego vehicle ACC should re-establish the time-gap with leader2. After the ego vehicle passes leader1, and if there is sufficient gap between leader1 and leader3 (which lies ahead of leader1 in the same lane), the ego vehicle switches back to its original lane. The ego vehicle ACC should then re-establish its time-gap with leader3.

5.4   ACC Test Objectives

The objective of testing all four uses cases, was to look for violations of two global safety requirements. The first was a basic no crash/collision requirement which is considered safety critical. The second safety requirement is that the observed time gap deviation should never vary by more than 20% of the selected time gap. We modeled these safety requirements in ROBOTest as follows:

```
verdict[i] = always(collision = false &
    timeGap <= 2.2 & timeGap >= 1.8)
```

6   Results

Each of the four use cases presented in Sect. 5.3 was formally modeled as an n-step sequence of input and gate constraints (for appropriate n) using the modeling language presented in Sect. 4. Each constraint model was then embedded into its own ROBOTest configuration file, and the safety requirements of Sect. 5.4 were added as verdict constraints. The configuration file was then run in a test session on the integrated ASM-ROBOTest toolchain. Table 1 shows the results of the four test sessions.

(a) Input test case									
Test vector#	TO1Vel	TO2Vel	TO3Vel	egoSteer	Test vector#	TO1Vel	TO2Vel	TO3Vel	egoSteer
1	50	55	50	0	10	50	60	50	0
2	50	55	50	0	11	50	70	50	0
3	50	55	50	left[100_2]	12	50	60	50	0
4	50	55	50	left[100_2]	13	50	50	50	right[100_2]
5	50	70	50	0	14	50	50	50	right[100_2]
6	50	70	50	0	15	0	50	40	0
7	50	70	50	0	16	0	50	30	0
8	50	70	50	0	17	0	50	30	0
9	50	70	50	0					

(b) Output observations										
Time (s)	collision	ego2TO1Dist	ego2TO2Dist	ego2TO3Dist	timeGap	accTarget	TO1Spd	TO2Spd	TO3Spd	egoSpd
0.0	False	0.0	0.0	0.0	0.0	0.0	0.0	0.0	0.0	0.0
1.0	False	38.1	39.4	68.1	1.8	1.0	50.0	55.0	50.0	77.2
2.0	False	31.9	31.6	61.9	1.7	1.0	50.0	55.0	50.0	67.2
3.0	False	28.9	33.0	58.9	0.0	0.0	50.0	55.0	50.0	55.9
4.0	False	27.9	33.5	57.9	0.0	0.0	50.0	55.0	50.0	54.4
5.0	False	25.3	36.3	55.3	0.0	0.0	50.0	70.0	50.0	64.7
6.0	False	20.0	36.5	50.0	1.8	2.0	50.0	70.0	50.0	71.3
7.0	False	14.2	36.3	44.2	1.8	2.0	50.0	70.0	50.0	70.7
8.0	False	8.5	36.1	38.5	1.9	2.0	50.0	70.0	50.0	70.2
9.0	False	3.0	36.2	33.0	1.9	2.0	50.0	70.0	50.0	69.8
10.0	False	-2.3	33.7	27.7	1.8	2.0	50.0	60.0	50.0	67.1
11.0	False	-6.4	35.1	23.6	2.0	2.0	50.0	70.0	50.0	63.9
12.0	False	-10.2	34.1	19.8	1.9	2.0	50.0	60.0	50.0	63.4
13.0	False	-13.6	30.9	16.4	0.0	0.0	50.0	50.0	50.0	60.8
14.0	False	-16.5	28.0	13.5	0.8	3.0	50.0	50.0	50.0	62.5
15.0	False	-33.2	24.8	7.6	0.5	3.0	0.0	50.0	40.0	58.9
16.0	False	-48.0	23.9	1.2	0.1	3.0	0.0	50.0	30.0	46.9
17.0	True	-59.1	26.6	-1.5	0.0	0.0	0.0	50.0	30.0	34.2

Fig. 2. A failed test case for the Overtaking Scenario 5.3: (a) test inputs from ROBOTest, (b) test outputs from ASM

Table 1 shows that errors were found in two of the four use cases. It was easy to visually inspect the failed test cases reported by ROBOTest and confirm that the safety requirements were indeed violated (c.f. Fig. 2(b)). Furthermore, failed test cases could be played back through the ASM simulator in real time to visualise the full details. Figure 2 shows a complete failed test case for overtaking, consisting of 17 test vectors for the 4 input parameters that drive a 17 s simulation. Still images from replaying this test case in ASM can be seen in Fig. 3, where the ego (i.e. ACC host) vehicle is dark blue. Figure 3(e) shows the collision in Step 5. Such visualisations can yield further explanatory insight into *why* a test failure occurs. In this case, the test failures were mainly collision errors when a sudden speed change occurred.

Although use case errors were found in the SUT, the models in Table 1 were not fully converged (i.e. learning was incomplete) This was due to the relatively low data throughput of a single simulator license. Further research is needed to evaluate whether multi-threaded machine learning, using more than one simulator, can achieve full convergence (i.e. a completely learned model) in a reasonable time.

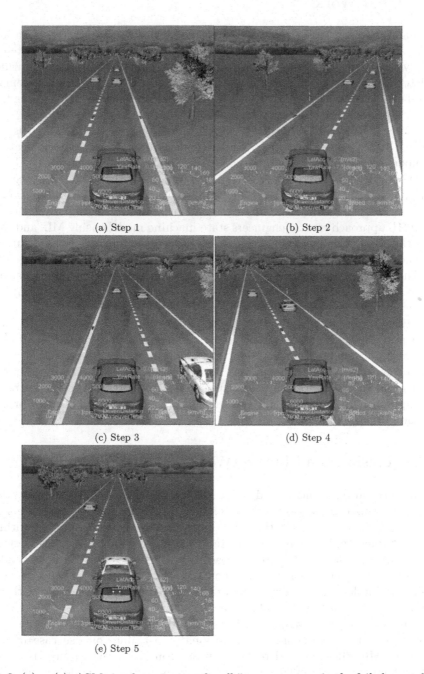

(a) Step 1   (b) Step 2

(c) Step 3   (d) Step 4

(e) Step 5

Fig. 3. (a),...,(e): ASM simulator images for all 5 use case steps in the failed overtaking use case test of Fig. 2 (Color figure online)

7   Related Work

Active automaton learning for testing is surveyed in [3], where the applications are mainly unit and integration testing. Our work represents the first attempt to apply ML to use case testing. The commonest models for automaton learning are deterministic automata [18,19,27,31,35], non-deterministic finite automata [5], and extended finite state machines [6]. Our work seems to represent the first attempt to use chains of intersecting finite automata.

There is a significant literature on TCG for use cases from UML models surveyed in [32]. UML sequence diagrams are sometimes seen as the canonical use case modeling language, and are prominent in the UML literature on TCG, e.g. [29]. The linear step ordering (see Sect. 2.1) common to both UML sequence diagrams [29] and informal models [8] is faithfully reflected in our CAML approach. UML state machine models are used in [33] for use case testing. By contrast, the CAML approach reverse engineers state machine models using ML, and thus avoids the effort of manual model construction and maintenance. Several authors have understood the need for constraints to automate use case testing e.g. [29], [24]. The UML object constraint language (OCL) has typically been used for this. By contrast, our constraints are based on linear temporal logic (LTL) and are conceptually closer to the live sequence charts of [16].

Testing semi- and fully autonomous vehicle software is a technically challenging emerging field where use case modeling languages such as OpenScenario [28] are currently under development. The case studies presented here extend previous research into automotive use case testing such as [4,25]. CAML addresses similar problems to the fuzz testing approach of [15]. However, our constraint-based approach to modeling and verdicts has wider scope and is more precise than the randomised approach of [15].

8   Conclusions and Future Work

We have introduced a constrained active machine learning (CAML) architecture that fully automates use case testing. This architecture can overcome the scalability problems associated with current active automaton learning algorithms such as L* when applied to highly constrained situations such as use case testing. We have benchmarked the CAML approach on typical use cases for an embedded automotive ADAS application, and demonstrated its efficiency and effectiveness. For this we implemented a prototype of CAML which was integrated with the industrial vehicle simulator ASM.

There is considerable scope for extension and improvement of our approach. Future research topics include: (i) additional constraints on use case models for greater ML efficiency and reduced automaton sizes, (ii) extensions of the constraint language for wider scope of use case and verdict modeling, and (iii) interfacing our constraint modeling language to open standards such as UML, LSC and OpenScenario.

Acknowledgement. We acknowledge the collaboration of Fengco AB in making available an ASM vehicle simulator license within the Vinnova funded project 2017-05501 Chronos-2. We also acknowledge the assistance of M. Höglund to connect CAML with ASM.

References

1. Angluin, D.: Learning regular sets from queries and counterexamples. Inf. Comput. **75**(2), 87–106 (1987)
2. Bennaceur, A., Hähnle, R., Meinke, K. (eds.): Machine Learning for Dynamic Software Analysis: Potentials and Limits. LNCS, vol. 11026. Springer, Cham (2018). https://doi.org/10.1007/978-3-319-96562-8
3. Bennaceur, A., Meinke, K.: Machine learning for software analysis: models, methods, and applications. In: Bennaceur, A., Hähnle, R., Meinke, K. (eds.) Machine Learning for Dynamic Software Analysis: Potentials and Limits. LNCS, vol. 11026, pp. 3–49. Springer, Cham (2018). https://doi.org/10.1007/978-3-319-96562-8_1
4. Bergenhem, C., Meinke, K., Ström, F.: Quantitative safety analysis of a coordinated emergency brake protocol for vehicle platoons. In: Margaria, T., Steffen, B. (eds.) ISoLA 2018, Part III. LNCS, vol. 11246, pp. 386–404. Springer, Cham (2018). https://doi.org/10.1007/978-3-030-03424-5_26
5. Bollig, B., Habermehl, P., Kern, C., Leucker, M.: Angluin-style learning of NFA. In: Boutilier, C. (ed.) IJCAI 2009, Proceedings of the 21st International Joint Conference on Artificial Intelligence, pp. 1004–1009 (2009)
6. Cassel, S., Howar, F., Jonsson, B., Steffen, B.: Active learning for extended finite state machines. Formal Asp. Comput. **28**(2), 233–216 (2016)
7. Clarke, E.M., Grumberg, O., Peled, D.A.: Model Checking. The MIT Press, Cambridge (2001)
8. Cockburn, A.: Writing Effective Use Cases, 1st edn. Addison-Wesley Longman Publishing Co. Inc., Boston (2000)
9. Cook, S., et al.: Unified modeling language (UML) version 2.5.1. Standard, Object Management Group (OMG), December 2017. https://www.omg.org/spec/UML/2.5.1
10. Fiterău-Broştean, P., Howar, F.: Learning-based testing the sliding window behavior of TCP implementations. In: Petrucci, L., Seceleanu, C., Cavalcanti, A. (eds.) FMICS/AVoCS 2017. LNCS, vol. 10471, pp. 185–200. Springer, Cham (2017). https://doi.org/10.1007/978-3-319-67113-0_12
11. Foster, D.: Generative Deep Learning: Teaching Machines To Paint, Write, Compose, and Play. O'Reilly, Sebastopol (2019)
12. Fournier, G.: Essential Software Testing. CRC Press, Boca Raton (2009). pB
13. Fowler, M.: UML Distilled: A Brief Guide to the Standard Object Modeling Language, 3rd edn. Addison-Wesley Longman Publishing Co., Inc., Boston (2003)
14. Gold, E.M.: Complexity of automaton identification from given data. Inf. Control **37**, 302–320 (1978)
15. Han, J.C., Zhou, Z.Q.: Metamorphic fuzz testing of autonomous vehicles. In: ICSEW 2020: Proceedings of the IEEE/ACM 42nd International Conference on Software Engineering Workshops. Association for Computing Machinery, New York (2020)
16. Harel, D., Marelly, R.: Come, Let's Play: Scenario-Based Programming Using LSC's and the Play-Engine. Springer, Heidelberg (2003). https://doi.org/10.1007/978-3-642-19029-2

17. De la Higuera, C.: Grammatical Inference: Learning Automata and Grammars. Cambridge University Press, New York (2010)
18. Hossen, K., Groz, R., Oriat, C., Richier, J.: Automatic model inference of web applications for security testing. In: Seventh IEEE International Conference on Software Testing, Verification and Validation, ICST 2014 Workshops Proceedings, Cleveland, Ohio, USA, March 31 - April 4 2014, pp. 22–23. IEEE Computer Society (2014). https://doi.org/10.1109/ICSTW.2014.47
19. Isberner, M., Howar, F., Steffen, B.: The TTT algorithm: a redundancy-free approach to active automata learning. In: Bonakdarpour, B., Smolka, S.A. (eds.) RV 2014. LNCS, vol. 8734, pp. 307–322. Springer, Cham (2014). https://doi.org/10.1007/978-3-319-11164-3_26
20. Jacobson, I., Magnus, C., Jonsson, P., Övergaard, G.: Object-Oriented Software Engineering: A Use Case Driven Approach. Addison Wesley Longman Publishing Co. Inc., Harlow (1992)
21. Kearns, M.J., Vazirani, U.V.: An Introduction to Computational Learning Theory. MIT Press, Cambridge (1994)
22. Khosrowjerdi, H., Meinke, K., Rasmusson, A.: Learning-based testing for safety critical automotive applications. In: Bozzano, M., Papadopoulos, Y. (eds.) IMBSA 2017. LNCS, vol. 10437, pp. 197–211. Springer, Cham (2017). https://doi.org/10.1007/978-3-319-64119-5_13
23. Khosrowjerdi, H., Meinke, K., Rasmusson, A.: Virtualized-fault injection testing: a machine learning approach. In: 11th IEEE International Conference on Software Testing, Verification and Validation, ICST 2018, Västerås, Sweden, 9–13 April 2018, pp. 297–308. IEEE Computer Society (2018). http://doi.ieeecomputersociety.org/10.1109/ICST.2018.00037
24. Li, B., Li, Z., Qing, L., Chen, Y.: Test case automate generation from UML sequence diagram and OCL expression. In: 2007 International Conference on Computational Intelligence and Security (CIS 2007), pp. 1048–1052 (2007)
25. Meinke, K.: Learning-based testing of cyber-physical systems-of-systems: a platooning study. In: Reinecke, P., Di Marco, A. (eds.) EPEW 2017. LNCS, vol. 10497, pp. 135–151. Springer, Cham (2017). https://doi.org/10.1007/978-3-319-66583-2_9
26. Meinke, K., Niu, F., Sindhu, M.: Learning-based software testing: a tutorial. In: Hähnle, R., Knoop, J., Margaria, T., Schreiner, D., Steffen, B. (eds.) ISoLA 2011. CCIS, pp. 200–219. Springer, Heidelberg (2012). https://doi.org/10.1007/978-3-642-34781-8_16
27. Meinke, K., Sindhu, M.A.: Incremental learning-based testing for reactive systems. In: Gogolla, M., Wolff, B. (eds.) TAP 2011. LNCS, vol. 6706, pp. 134–151. Springer, Heidelberg (2011). https://doi.org/10.1007/978-3-642-21768-5_11
28. Menzel, T., Bagschik, G., Isensee, L., Schomburg, A., Maurer, M.: From functional to logical scenarios: detailing a keyword-based scenario description for execution in a simulation environment. In: 2019 IEEE Intelligent Vehicles Symposium, IV 2019, Paris, France, 9–12 June 2019, pp. 2383–2390. IEEE (2019)
29. Nayak, A., Samanta, D.: Automatic test data synthesis using UML sequence diagrams. J. Object Technol. 9(2), 115–144 (2010)
30. Peled, D.A., Vardi, M.Y., Yannakakis, M.: Black box checking. In: Formal Methods for Protocol Engineering and Distributed Systems, FORTE XII/PSTV XIX'99, IFIP TC6 WG6.1, pp. 225–240 (1999)
31. Raffelt, H., Steffen, B., Margaria, T.: Dynamic testing via automata learning. In: Yorav, K. (ed.) HVC 2007. LNCS, vol. 4899, pp. 136–152. Springer, Heidelberg (2008). https://doi.org/10.1007/978-3-540-77966-7_13

32. Shirole, M., Kumar, R.: UML behavioral model based test case generation: a survey. SIGSOFT Softw. Eng. Notes **38**(4), 1–13 (2013)
33. Shirole, M., Suthar, A., Kumar, R.: Generation of improved test cases from UML state diagram using genetic algorithm. In: Proceedings of the 4th India Software Engineering Conference, pp. 125–134 (2011)
34. Vasilevski, M.P.: Failure diagnosis of automata. Cybernetic **9**(4), 653–665 (1973)
35. Walkinshaw, N., Bogdanov, K., Derrick, J., Paris, J.: Increasing functional coverage by inductive testing: a case study. In: Petrenko, A., Simão, A., Maldonado, J.C. (eds.) ICTSS 2010. LNCS, vol. 6435, pp. 126–141. Springer, Heidelberg (2010). https://doi.org/10.1007/978-3-642-16573-3_10
36. Wong, P., et al.: Testing abstract behavioral specifications. Int. J. Softw. Tools Technol. Transf. **17**(1), 107–119 (2015)
37. Özguner, U., Acarman, T., Redmill, K.: Autonomous Ground Vehicles. Artech House Publishers, Boston (2011)

Architecture-Guided Test Resource Allocation via Logic

Clovis Eberhart[1,2(✉)] [iD], Akihisa Yamada[3] [iD], Stefan Klikovits[1] [iD],
Shin-ya Katsumata[1] [iD], Tsutomu Kobayashi[1,4] [iD], Ichiro Hasuo[1] [iD],
and Fuyuki Ishikawa[1] [iD]

[1] National Institute of Informatics, 2-1-2 Hitotsubashi, Chiyoda-ku,
Tokyo 101-8430, Japan
{eberhart,klikovits,s-katsumata,t-kobayashi,hasuo,f-ishikawa}@nii.ac.jp
[2] Japanese-French Laboratory for Informatics, Tokyo, Japan
[3] National Institute of Advanced Industrial Science and Technology, 2-3-26, Aomi,
Koto-ku, Tokyo 135-0064, Japan
akihisa.yamada@aist.go.jp
[4] Japan Science and Technology Agency, 4-1-8, Honcho,
Kawaguchi-shi, Saitama 332-0012, Japan

Abstract. We introduce a new logic named Quantitative Confidence Logic (QCL) that quantifies the level of confidence one has in the conclusion of a proof. By translating a fault tree representing a system's architecture to a proof, we show how to use QCL to give a solution to the test resource allocation problem that takes the given architecture into account. We implemented a tool called `Astrahl` and compared our results to other testing resource allocation strategies.

Keywords: Reliability · Test resources allocation · Logic

1 Introduction

With modern systems growing in size and complexity, asserting their correctness has become a paramount task, and despite advances in the area of formal verification, testing remains a vital part of the system life cycle due to its versatility, practicality, and low entry barrier. Nevertheless, as test resources are limited, it is an important task to most effectively allocate them among system components, a problem commonly known as the test resource allocation problem (TRAP) (see e.g. [12]). In this paper we formulate the TRAP as follows: given a system that consists of multiple components and a certain, limited amount of test resources (e. g. time or money), how much of the budget should we allocate to each component in order to minimise the chance of system failure, i. e. to increase its reliability.

The authors are supported by ERATO HASUO Metamathematics for Systems Design Project (No. JPMJER1603).

F. Loulergue and F. Wotawa (Eds.): TAP 2021, LNCS 12740, pp. 22–38, 2021.
https://doi.org/10.1007/978-3-030-79379-1_2

We propose an approach to the TRAP, based on a novel logic system called Quantitative Confidence Logic (QCL). QCL differs from classical logic, in that a proof tree does not conclude truth from assumptions, but rather analyses how *confidence* is propagated from assumptions to conclusions. We prove key soundness properties of QCL with respect to a probabilistic interpretation (Sect. 2).

Learning a new logic is a hard task, especially to practitioners. Thus we do not demand users to learn QCL, but take it as an intermediate language to which already accepted representations of system architectures are translated. As an example, we show how to translate the well-known concept of fault trees (FTs) into QCL proof trees (Sect. 3).

We then formulate the TRAP as an optimisation problem with respect to a given FT, translated to a QCL proof tree (Sect. 4). Here we allow users to specify a *confidence function* for each component, which describes how an amount of spent test resources relates to an increase in that component's reliability.

We implement our approach as a tool (`Astrahl`) that takes as input an FT, a confidence function for each component, the current confidence in each component, and the total amount of test resources the user plans to spend. Then `Astrahl` outputs a proposed allocation of the test resources over components. We validate our approach through experiments (Sect. 5).

An advantage of our method is that it is not tied to a fixed confidence function, and can therefore assign different confidence functions to different components. This will be useful in modelling systems with highly heterogeneous components such as cyber-physical systems (CPSs); for example, hardware components would demand more effort to increase confidence than software, and would depend on the type of components or their vendors.

We expect `Astrahl` to be used continuously in a system's development: the confidence in each component increases as they pass more tests. By rerunning `Astrahl` with updated component confidences, we obtain a test resource allocation strategy. We expect our approach to be promising in product line development, where a number of system configurations are simultaneously developed with common components. In such a situation, updating confidence in a component for one system positively impacts the test strategies for other systems.

1.1   Related Work

Test Resource Allocation. Most approaches to the TRAP use software reliability growth models (SRGMs) such as models based on Poisson Process (e. g. [7]) to capture the relationship between testing efforts and reliability growth, or in our words, confidence functions. A typical TRAP approach formulates the problem using a particular SRGM and provides a solution using exact optimisation [10] or a metaheuristic such as a genetic algorithm [19]. A challenge in this area is to take the structure (inter-module relations) of the target system into account; existing studies consider particular structures such as parallel-series architecture [19] or Markovian architecture [13]. In addition, there is high demand for dynamic allocation methods (e. g. [3]) because in practice SRGMs, system structures, and testing processes often become different from those planned at first. Our approach has multiple beneficial features over the existing approaches: (1) it is independent of particular SRGMs and optimisation strategies, (2) it can take complex structure into account using FTs, and (3) it can be used for dynamic allocation.

Fuzzy Logics. Fuzzy logics [8] is a branch of logic interested in deductions where Boolean values are too coarse. In its standard semantics [6], formulas are given a numeric truth value in the interval $[0, 1]$, where 0 represents falsity and 1 truth. These numerical values can be used to represent the confidence one has in an assertion: we give high values to propositions we are confident are true, and low values to those we are confident are false. This is slightly different from our approach, where 1 corresponds to confidence (either in truth or falsity) and 0 to absence of knowledge.

Dempster-Shafer Theory. Dempster-Shafer theory [4,15] is a mathematical theory of belief. One of its characteristic features is that if one has a belief b in an assertion, they can have any belief $b' \leq 1 - b$ in its negation, contrary to traditional Bayesian models, where it is necessarily $1 - b$. This feature is crucial to model uncertainty due to absence of knowledge, and Dempster-Shafer theory has been used to model reliability in engineering contexts [14]. Our approach draws inspiration from fuzzy and three-valued logics to model this feature.

Fault Tree Analysis. Fault trees [17] are tree structures that represent how faults propagate through a system. In qualitative FT analysis, they are used to determine root causes [5]. In quantitative FT analysis, basic events are assigned fault probabilities, and the overall system failure probability is given by propagating the fault probabilities through the fault tree. Our approach uses the same ingredients (assigning numeric values to basic events and propagating them through the fault tree), but repurposed to solve another problem.

2   Quantitative Confidence Logic

This section introduces QCL, which we use throughout this paper. A QCL formula is a standard propositional formula φ equipped with a pair of reals, written $\varphi: (t, f)$, where $t \in [0, 1]$ represents our confidence that φ holds and $f \in [0, 1]$ the confidence that φ does not hold, so $t + f$ represents how much confidence one has about φ, and $1 - t - f$ lack of confidence about φ. Absolute confidence is represented by 1 and total absence of knowledge by 0, so that $\varphi: (1, 0)$ means full trust that φ holds, $\varphi: (0, 0)$ means we have no knowledge about φ, and $\varphi: (1/2, 1/2)$ represents the fact that we know with very high confidence that φ holds with 50% chance.

In Sect. 2.1 we define the syntax of QCL and introduce its proof rules. We also show how to derive standard proof rules from them. In Sect. 2.2 we give a probabilistic interpretation of QCL formulas and show that QCL proof rules are sound with respect to it. We also explain how the particular shapes of the rules serve as the basis of our optimisation algorithm (Sect. 4).

2.1 Syntax and Proof Rules of QCL

This section introduces QCL, starting with *formulas with confidences*, then sequents, and finally proof rules.

Definition 1. *Given an arbitrary set of atomic propositions* Prop, *formulas are defined inductively by the following grammar:*

$$\varphi ::= A \mid \top \mid \bot \mid \varphi \Rightarrow \varphi,$$

for $A \in$ Prop. We denote by Form *the set of all formulas.*

As in classical logic, negation, disjunction, and conjunction can be defined by syntactic sugar $\neg\varphi \equiv \varphi \Rightarrow \bot$, $\varphi \vee \psi \equiv \neg\varphi \Rightarrow \psi$, and $\varphi \wedge \psi \equiv \neg(\neg\varphi \vee \neg\psi)$.

We now equip such formulas with confidence. We define the *space of confidences* as $\mathbb{C} = \{(t, f) \in [0,1]^2 \mid t + f \leq 1\}$.

Definition 2. *A formula with confidence is a pair $(\varphi, c) \in$ Form $\times \mathbb{C}$, written $\varphi : c$. For $\varphi : (t, f)$, we call t the* true confidence *in φ and f its* false confidence.

Intuitively, a formula with confidence $\varphi : (t, f)$ represents the fact that our confidence that φ holds is t, and our confidence that φ does not hold is f. This should mean that the chance that φ holds is at least t, and the chance that it does not is at least f. Another way to look at confidences is *intervals of probability*. Each confidence (t, f) bijectively determines a sub-interval $[t, 1 - f]$ of $[0, 1]$. Then a formula with confidence $\varphi : (t, f)$ represents that the probability of φ being true is within the interval $[t, 1-f]$. We make this intuition more concrete in Sect. 2.2, where we give an interpretation of QCL in terms of probabilities.

Equipping formulas with numeric values is reminiscent of fuzzy logics[1]. To explain the fundamental difference between our approach and fuzzy logics, let us consider two orders on $\mathbb{C}$. Let $(t, f) \sqsubseteq (t', f')$ if $t \leq t'$ and $f \leq f'$; we call $\sqsubseteq$ the *confidence order*, as $c \sqsubseteq c'$ holds exactly when c' represents more confidence (both true and false) than c. Our approach is centred around $\sqsubseteq$, since we are interested in "how confident" we are in an assertion. Similarly, let $(t, f) \leq (t', f')$ if $t \leq t'$ and $f \geq f'$; we call $\leq$ the *truth order*, as $c \leq c'$ intuitively means that c' is "more true" than c. Fuzzy logics is centred around the truth order $\leq$ (especially on elements of the form $(t, 1 - t)$), as it is a logic about how true assertions are.

One way to link our approach to fuzzy logics is via three-valued logics [1]. Fuzzy logics can be seen as equipping formulas with a numeric truth value $t \in [0, 1]$ and a falsity value $f \in [0, 1]$ such that $t + f = 1$. This is equivalent to equipping formulas only with a numeric value $t \in [0, 1]$, while f is the implicit difference to 1. With three-valued logics, formulas have three possible outcomes: truth $\top$, falsity $\bot$, and uncertainty $\mathbb{I}$, and each is given a value t, f, and u, such

---

[1] Here, we mean fuzzy logics interpreted in $[0, 1]$.

that $t + f + u = 1$, which is equivalent to equipping them with $(t, f) \in [0, 1]^2$ such that $t + f \leq 1$, while u is implicit. Dempster-Shafer theory is similar, with t representing our belief in φ, f our belief in $\neg\varphi$, and u our degree of uncertainty.

We now introduce the sequents on which QCL operates.

Definition 3. *A sequent in QCL, written $\Gamma \vdash \varphi \colon c$, consists of a finite set $\Gamma \subseteq$ Form $\times\, \mathbb{C}$ of formulas with confidences (written as a list), a formula $\varphi \in$ Form, and a confidence $c \in \mathbb{C}$.*

Such a sequent intuitively means that, if all formulas with corresponding confidences in Γ hold, then φ holds with confidence c as well.

$$\frac{}{\Gamma, \varphi \colon (t, f) \vdash \varphi \colon (t, f)}\ (ax) \qquad \frac{}{\Gamma \vdash \varphi \colon (0, 0)}\ (unk) \qquad \frac{}{\Gamma \vdash \top \colon (1, 0)}\ (\top_{\mathrm{I}})$$

$$\frac{}{\Gamma \vdash \bot \colon (0, 1)}\ (\bot_{\mathrm{I}}) \qquad \frac{\Gamma \vdash \varphi \colon (t, f) \qquad \Gamma \vdash \psi \colon (t', f')}{\Gamma \vdash \varphi \Rightarrow \psi \colon (f + t' - ft', tf')}\ (\Rightarrow_{\mathrm{I}})$$

$$\frac{\Gamma \vdash \varphi \Rightarrow \psi \colon (t, f) \qquad \Gamma \vdash \varphi \colon (t', f')}{\Gamma \vdash \psi \colon \left(1 - \dfrac{1 - t}{t'}, \dfrac{f}{1 - f'}\right)}\ (\Rightarrow_{\mathrm{E},l})\ \text{if } t' \neq 0 \text{ and } f' \neq 1$$

$$\frac{\Gamma \vdash \varphi \Rightarrow \psi \colon (t, f) \qquad \Gamma \vdash \psi \colon (t', f')}{\Gamma \vdash \varphi \colon \left(\dfrac{f}{1 - t'}, 1 - \dfrac{1 - t}{f'}\right)}\ (\Rightarrow_{\mathrm{E},r})\ \text{if } t' \neq 1 \text{ and } f' \neq 0$$

Fig. 1. Proof rules of Quantitative Confidence Logic

Definition 4. *Proof trees in QCL are built from the QCL proofs rules given in Fig. 1. There, the notation $\chi \colon (t'', f'')$ in conclusions is a shorthand for*

$$\chi \colon (\min(\max(t'', 0), 1), \min(\max(f'', 0), 1)).$$

Note that $(t'', f'') \in \mathbb{C}$ because $t'' + f'' \leq 1$ in all rules. Note also that rules $(\Rightarrow_{\mathrm{E},l})$ and $(\Rightarrow_{\mathrm{E},r})$ are conditioned so that confidence values do not contain indeterminate forms $0/0$. These side conditions correspond to the facts that, if $\varphi \Rightarrow \psi$ is true, φ being false gives no information about ψ, and ψ being true gives no information about φ.

(ax), $(\top_{\mathrm{I}})$, and $(\bot_{\mathrm{I}})$ are self-explanatory, while (unk) states that anything can be proved, but with null confidence. One way to think about $(\Rightarrow_{\mathrm{I}})$ is that, if φ and ψ are independent (in a way made precise in Sect. 2.2), φ holds with probability in $[t, 1 - f]$ and ψ with probability in $[t', 1 - f']$, then $\varphi \Rightarrow \psi$ holds with probability in $[f + t' - ft', tf']$. The elimination rules are designed similarly.

From the rules in Fig. 1 and the encodings of negation, disjunction, and conjunction, we can derive the introduction rules in Fig. 2 (we can also derive

$$\frac{\Gamma \vdash \varphi : (t, f)}{\Gamma \vdash \neg\varphi : (f, t)} \ (\neg_I) \qquad \frac{\Gamma \vdash \varphi : (t, f) \qquad \Gamma \vdash \psi : (t', f')}{\Gamma \vdash \varphi \wedge \psi : (tt', f + f' - ff')} \ (\wedge_I)$$

$$\frac{\Gamma \vdash \varphi : (t, f) \qquad \Gamma \vdash \psi : (t', f')}{\Gamma \vdash \varphi \vee \psi : (t + t' - tt', ff')} \ (\vee_I)$$

Fig. 2. Derivable introduction rules

elimination rules, but do not discuss them here). A point worth attention is that the shape of these rules is quite unorthodox. In particular, one should not need to have confidence in both disjuncts to have confidence in a disjunction. However, this unorthodox shape is exactly the reason why our solution to the TRAP (defined in Sect. 4) works well, as we show in Example 16. Moreover, we can derive a disjunction from a single disjunct, as:

$$\frac{\Gamma \vdash \varphi : (t, f) \qquad \dfrac{}{\Gamma \vdash \psi : (0, 0)} \ (unk)}{\Gamma \vdash \varphi \vee \psi : (t + 0 - t \cdot 0, f \cdot 0) = (t, 0)} \ (\vee_I),$$

which represents (one of) the usual disjunction introduction rules.

Remark 5. QCL rules are different from those of classical logic and do not extend them. Because the rules' design is strongly centred around how confidence flows from hypotheses to conclusions and based on independence of hypotheses, QCL cannot prove sequents such as $\emptyset \vdash A \Rightarrow A : (1, 0)$. How to allow reasoning about both confidence and truth in the same logic is left for future work.

Example 6. The correctness of a system with software and hardware components is based on the correctness of both components. A classical logical proof that the system is correct assuming both its software and hardware are correct is:

$$\frac{\dfrac{}{\Gamma \vdash \text{software}} \ (ax) \qquad \dfrac{}{\Gamma \vdash \text{hardware}} \ (ax)}{\Gamma \vdash \text{software} \wedge \text{hardware}} \ (\wedge_I),$$

where $\Gamma = \{\text{software}, \text{hardware}\}$. By adding confidence to the formulas, we derive confidence in the assertion that the whole system is correct as a QCL proof:

$$\frac{\dfrac{}{\Gamma \vdash \text{software} : (0.5, 0.2)} \ (ax) \qquad \dfrac{}{\Gamma \vdash \text{hardware} : (0.3, 0.01)} \ (ax)}{\Gamma \vdash \text{software} \wedge \text{hardware} : (0.15, 0.208)} \ (\wedge_I).$$

If we assume the software system is built from components that are difficult to prove reliable (e.g. machine learning algorithms), but much testing effort has been spent on it, then both true and false confidence may be high, as in the example above. On the contrary, if there are no reasons not to trust the hardware (e.g. it is made of very simple, reliable components), but less testing effort has been spent on it, then both true and false confidence may be lower than those of the software system.

It may seem unnecessary to keep track of false confidence, since our ultimate goal is to prove system reliability (and not unreliability). However, there are several cases in which we may want to use it. For instance, the calculation of how often a volatile system fails can be translated to a false confidence problem. Moreover, systems with failsafe mechanisms, e.g. *if A works, use module B, else use module C*, need to take the unreliability of A into account. Otherwise, the whole system's reliability could not be correctly expressed, as it would only depend on A and B. Hence, the optimisation would ignore the reliability of C.

Remark 7. In Fig. 2, negation is an involution, and the reader familiar with fuzzy logics will have noticed the product T-norm and its dual probabilistic sum T-conorm in the rules $(\wedge_I)$ and $(\vee_I)$. Negation is an involution of $[0, 1]$ in fuzzy logics, and T-norms and T-conorms are the standard interpretations of conjunction and disjunction in fuzzy logics, which hints at a deep connection between our approach and fuzzy logics. However, implication is not interpreted as a residual, which again differentiates our approach from fuzzy logics.

2.2   Interpretation as Random Variables

In this section, we justify the QCL proof rules by giving formulas a probabilistic semantics and showing that these rules are sound.

We start with some measure-theoretic conventions. We write 2 to mean the discrete measurable space over the two-point set $\mathbb{B} = \{\top, \bot\}$. Boolean algebraic operations over 2 are denoted by $\wedge, \Rightarrow$, etc. (There should be no possible confusion with formulas.) For a probability space $(\Omega, \mathfrak{F}, P)$ (or Ω for short), $\mathrm{Meas}(\Omega, 2)$ denotes the set of 2-valued random variables. A *context* is a Prop-indexed family of 2-valued random variables, given as a function $\rho\colon \mathrm{Prop} \to \mathrm{Meas}(\Omega, 2)$.

Definition 8. *Given a space* $(\Omega, \mathfrak{F}, P)$*, we inductively extend a context* ρ *to a Form-indexed family of 2-valued random variables* $\bar{\rho}\colon \mathrm{Form} \to \mathrm{Meas}(\Omega, 2)$*:*

$$\bar{\rho}(A) = \rho(A), \quad \bar{\rho}(\top)(x) = \top, \quad \bar{\rho}(\bot)(x) = \bot, \quad \bar{\rho}(\varphi \Rightarrow \psi)(x) = \bar{\rho}(\varphi)(x) \Rightarrow \bar{\rho}(\psi)(x).$$

The semantics $\llbracket\varphi\rrbracket_{\Omega,\rho}$ *of a formula* φ *in a space* Ω *and context* ρ *is defined to be the probability* $P[\bar{\rho}(\varphi) = \top]$ *of* φ *being true under* ρ*. We say that* $\varphi\colon (t, f)$ *holds in* Ω *and* ρ *if* $\llbracket\varphi\rrbracket_{\Omega,\rho} \in [t, 1-f]$*. We say that a sequent* $\Gamma \vdash \varphi\colon c$ *holds in* Ω *and* ρ*, if* $\varphi\colon c$ *holds in* Ω *and* ρ *whenever all* $\psi\colon c'$ *in* Γ *hold in* Ω *and* ρ*.*

In other words, the semantics of φ is the measure of the space on which φ holds, and $\varphi\colon (t, f)$ holds if φ is true on at least t of the space and false on at least f.

From here on, we only consider *independent* contexts, i.e. ρ's such that the random variables $\rho(A)$ are mutually independent for all atomic propositions A.

The following lemma lifts independence of ρ to $\bar{\rho}$.

Lemma 9. *Let* Ω *be a space and* ρ *an independent context. If* φ *and* ψ *share no atomic propositions, then for all* $S, T \subseteq \mathbb{B}$*, the following holds:*

$$P[\bar{\rho}(\varphi) \in S \wedge \bar{\rho}(\psi) \in T] = P[\bar{\rho}(\varphi) \in S]P[\bar{\rho}(\psi) \in T].$$

Proof. By strengthening the proposition to finitely many φ's and ψ's, then by induction on: max depth of φ's, number of φ's of max depth, max depth of ψ's, and number of ψ's of max depth (with lexicographic order).

We can finally prove soundness of the rules.

Lemma 10. *For all rules in Fig. 1, formulas φ and ψ that share no atomic propositions, spaces Ω, and independent contexts ρ, if the premise sequents hold in Ω and ρ, then so does the conclusion.*

Proof. Simple computations relying on Lemma 9.

Corollary 11. *If φ is linear (each atomic proposition appears at most once) and a proof π of $\Gamma \vdash \varphi\colon c$ only uses base rules and introduction rules, then $\Gamma \vdash \varphi\colon c$ holds in all spaces Ω and independent contexts ρ.*

3   Translating System Architectures to Proofs

In this section, we translate FTs [17] to QCL proof trees. This allows us to use a system's architecture—modelled as an FT—in our solution to the TRAP. The way this translation works is close to quantitative fault tree analysis, where FTs are equipped with fault probabilities. In our translation, these fault probabilities are translated to confidences in QCL proofs.

Definition 12. *A fault tree is a tree whose leaves are called* basic events, *and whose nodes, called* gate events, *are either* AND *or* OR *gates.*

Basic events represent independent components of a system, and the tree structure represents how faults propagate through the system. The system fails if faults propagate through the root node. The usual definition of fault trees is more general than the one we give here, but we use this one for simplicity.

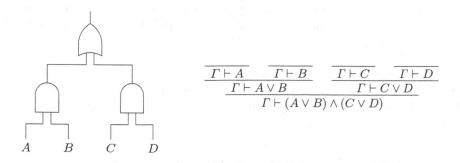

Fig. 3. A fault tree and its translation as a proof tree

Example 13. The FT in Fig. 3a represents a system composed of four basic components A, B, C, and D. For a fault to propagate through the system and become a failure, either both A and B have to fail, or both C and D (e.g., A and B could be redundant components, doubled to increase reliability).

In *quantitative fault tree analysis* [5], failure probabilities are assigned to basic events, and they propagate through event gates as if mutually independent. In other words, if the failure probabilities of an AND gate's inputs are a and b, then its output failure probability is ab, and $a + b - ab$ for an OR gate.

We translate fault trees to QCL proof trees as follows: The set Prop of atomic propositions collects all the names of basic events. Γ consists of A: (t_A, f_A) for each $A \in$ Prop. AND gates are translated to $(\vee_I)$ rules, and OR gates to $(\wedge_I)$ rules.

The reason for this dualisation is straightforward: while a fault tree represents how faults propagate, proof trees represent confidence in a system's reliability, i.e., how *absence of faults* propagates: the true confidence in each atomic proposition in Γ now represents reliability of the component, and the true confidence in the conclusion represents reliability of the whole system.

Example 14. The translation of the fault tree of Fig. 3a is shown in Fig. 3b (with confidences left out for readability). Here, Prop $= \{A, B, C, D\}$ and the true confidence in the conclusion of the proof is $t_A t_B + t_C t_D - t_A t_B t_C t_D$. We can thus link increases in the reliability of components to increases in reliability of the whole system.

Note that the translation of a fault tree only uses base rules and introduction rules (more precisely, only (ax), $(\wedge_I)$, and $(\vee_I)$). This is partly because we only consider AND and OR gates, but more essentially, basic events of fault trees are considered atomic and thus there is no need to eliminate logical connectives. Moreover, an assignment of failure probabilities to basic events translates to a context ρ in QCL terms. Since all basic events are considered independent in an FT, their translation gives an independent context ρ. Therefore, the translation of a fault tree always verifies Corollary 11, and our interpretation as a QCL proof tree is sound for any assignment of failure probabilities to basic events. This means that, if the confidence in all basic components corresponds to their reliability, then the confidence of the whole proof cannot overshoot the whole system's reliability.

Since we translate fault probabilities to confidences, and fault probabilities are directly linked to reliability, we may use "reliability" and "confidence" interchangeably in the following, e.g. when we feel that reliability conveys a better intuition than confidence.

4   Solving the Test Resource Allocation Problem

In this section, we show how to optimise confidence in the conclusion of a QCL proof. This gives a solution to the TRAP through the translation of FTs to QCL proofs that was described in Sect. 3.

In order for this approach to be usable in practice, the user has to be able to specify two input parameters: the FT that represents the system's architecture, and functions describing how confidence in each component's reliability grows by spending resource on it. FTs are commonly used in the industry, so modelling a system using them should be no problem in practice. We first describe the latter input parameter in Sect. 4.1 and then give our solution to the TRAP in Sect. 4.2.

4.1   Confidence Functions

Increasing confidence in a proof's conclusion requires an increase in its premises' confidences. The cost of increasing confidence may vary among premises; when thinking in terms of systems (rather than proofs), for instance, increasing trust in a machine learning algorithm may require more effort than improving hardware reliability. This is a well-known problem, for which many solutions have been designed, especially SRGMs, which are based on mathematical modelling of faults [18]. Here, however, we do not choose a particular fault model and instead introduce the following abstract notion, which makes the approach versatile.

Definition 15. *A* confidence function *is a non-decreasing function* $f : \mathbb{R}_+ \to \mathbb{C}$ *(equipped with $\sqsubseteq$).*

The equality $f(r) = c$ means that after spending r resources on a formula, one will have confidence c in the formula. The monotonicity condition above enforces that, by spending more resources, confidence should not decrease.

Note that $f(0)$ can be different from $(0,0)$, which corresponds to the fact that engineers usually have some confidence in the components they use. This feature also makes it easy to use our approach in continuous development, by using confidence functions $f_s(r) = f(r + s)$ where s is the amount of resource that has been already spent to test a component.

Note also that a confidence function may increase the false confidence, theoretically capturing the fact that faults may found by testing. For an application on the TRAP, however, we assume that faults will be fixed and thus false confidence always stays at 0. In the following, we thus define confidence functions as increasing functions $f \colon \mathbb{R}_+ \to [0,1]$, which represents the true confidence, and assume the false confidence is always 0.

Designing Confidence Functions. Of course, expert knowledge on a component can be used to give a good estimate of confidence functions, but other techniques, such as *defect prediction* [11], exist for when knowledge is limited.

When testing is the canonical way to increase confidence, notions of test coverage serve as a good estimate of confidence. If we have a hardware test suite of n tests that achieves 100% coverage (but not enough budget to execute them all), and each test costs r_0 resources, then the coverage achieved by spending r resources in testing can be estimated as the confidence $f(r) = \min(r/nr_0, 1)$.

If we do not have such a test suite, then a reasonable way to model confidence is to assume uniform random testing. There we assume that each test covers a randomly sampled fraction p of the input space, but parts of it might be already covered by previous tests. If running a test costs r_0 resources, then a good estimate of confidence function is $f(r) = 1 - (1 - p)^{r/r_0}$.

If more is known about the component, then it is possible to design confidence functions that are better suited for this component. In particular, if we have some *a priori* knowledge about fault distributions, then it is possible to use SRGMs [18] as confidence functions.

4.2   The Optimisation Problem

We now formulate the TRAP as an optimisation problem in terms of QCL as follows: given a QCL proof, a confidence function for each premise, and a resource budget to spend, how should we spend the budget on the different premises to maximise confidence in the proof's conclusion?

We only consider the problem of optimising true confidence because the application we are aiming at is about reliability. However, with the same ingredients, we could define similar optimisation problems. For example, we could try to optimise total confidence $t + f$ under limited resources, or try to minimise resources spent to reach a given confidence objective (either in true or total confidence).

We begin with a simple observation: if $\varphi_1 : c_1, \ldots, \varphi_n : c_n \vdash \varphi : c$ is provable, then c is a non-decreasing function of the c_i's (for the confidence order $\sqsubseteq$). Hence, increases in the c_i's confidence lead to increases in c.

Because, for the translation of an FT, the true confidence of the conclusion has to be a function $f(t_1, \ldots, t_n)$ of the true confidences of the hypotheses, if the confidence of each hypothesis is given by applying a confidence function f_i to an amount of resources r_i spent on that hypothesis, then the true confidence of the conclusion is itself a function $f(f_1(r_1), \ldots, f_n(r_n))$ of the amount of resources spent on the hypotheses.

The problem is thus the following: given an initial condition $r_1, \ldots, r_n$, confidence functions $f_1, \ldots, f_n$, a proof of $\{\varphi_i : (c_i, 0) \mid i \in n\} \vdash \varphi : (f(c_1, \ldots, c_n), -)$, and a budget r, maximise $f(f_1(r_1 + r_1'), \ldots, f_n(r_n + r_n'))$ under $r_i' \geq 0$ for all $i \in n$ and $\sum_{i \in n} r_1' \leq r$.

We thus reduce the TRAP to a classic constrained optimisation problem, which we can solve using well-known algorithms. In our implementation, we use simulated annealing [16], but any other method (such as CMA-ES [9] or Lagrange multipliers [2]) would work too.

Example 16. Take the QCL proof from Example 13. Suppose that the confidence functions of components follow $f(r) = 1 - 1/2^r$, the amount of resources already spent on the components are 0 for A, 5 for B and C, and 10 for D, and we have a test resource budget of 10. Then we want to maximise

$$(1 - 1/2^a)(1 - 1/2^{5+b}) + (1 - 1/2^{5+c})(1 - 1/2^{10+d})$$
$$- (1 - 1/2^a)(1 - 1/2^{5+b})(1 - 1/2^{5+c})(1 - 1/2^{10+d})$$

under the constraints $a, b, c, d \geq 0$, and $a + b + c + d \leq 10$. There are two major points to note here. First, due to the fact that $(\vee_I)$ requires both disjuncts to be proved, the optimisation will try to increase confidence of *both* A and B, rather than choose one. Second, since we take system structure into accounr, the algorithm can give B and C different budgets, even though they share the same initial confidence and confidence function.

Our approach has significant advantages over other TRAP solutions. First, it makes use of the system's architecture, which is not the case of most approaches. Even other approaches that take system architecture into account generally only consider simple architectures, such as *parallel-series architecture* [19]. These architectures can be directly translated to FTs, but the converse is not possible without duplicating modules, which puts artificial weight to these duplicated modules. Moreover, we explained how to convert an FT to a QCL proof, but our algorithm is not limited to FTs and would work on other proofs.

Another advantage of our method is that it is not tied to any specific confidence function. The main advantage of this generality is that it allows the user to pick different confidence functions for different components. In particular, this approach should be helpful when allocating test resources for CPSs, where some components are software, while others are hardware, which most likely require to be modelled using different confidence functions.

5   Experimental Results

In this section, we describe the results of our experiments, showing that our tool `Astrahl`[2] can increase system reliability more consistently than others. To demonstrate the tool's performance, we designed two experiments. The first one compares `Astrahl`'s confidence gain to other test resource allocation (TRA) strategies. The second, more involved experiment tests whether the increase in confidence provided by `Astrahl` is linked to an increase in system reliability. Given an FT and confidence functions, we simulate existence of component faults, before splitting a fixed testing budget according to different TRA strategies (one of which is our approach). We then mimic component testing according to the allocated budget and fix faults if they are found, thereby increasing system reliability. Our evaluation repeats the probabilistic process to test which method gives the best reliability on average.

We developed `Astrahl`, which implements the TRA algorithm described in Sect. 4. It takes as input JSON descriptions of the fault tree and the confidence functions (as parse trees), an initial condition (a float for each basic event), and a budget (a float), and returns a splitting of the budget between the different basic events (a float for each basic event).

This section evaluates our claims and analyses `Astrahl`'s system confidence gains to other, more naive approaches. We first ask how much confidence we can gain by using `Astrahl`, rather than simpler TRA approaches. Then, we test whether using `Astrahl` can increase system reliability in practice. Specifically, this section will investigate the following two research questions:

---

[2] The code and experimental data are publicly available on https://github.com/ERATOMMSD/qcl_tap_2021.

RQ1 Given a certain TRA budget, how much is the calculated confidence gain when using `Astrahl` and how do these figures compare to alternative TRA methods?

RQ2 Does `Astrahl`'s gain in confidence translate to a gain in system reliability in a practical scenario where testing practice is simulated?

Alternative TRA Approaches. There exist numerous solutions to test resource splitting, however some of the most common ones are the uniform and proportional resource allocation strategies (see Fig. 4), as they do not require knowledge of the system structure or fault distribution. *Uniform* TRA, for instance, evenly distributes the available resources among the candidate components. This technique is completely agnostic of the current system and component confidences. *Proportional* TRA on the other hand aims to take current component confidence into account and provide proportionally more resources to components in which we have lower confidence. Although it uses current confidences for resource allocation, the system's structure is still not considered.

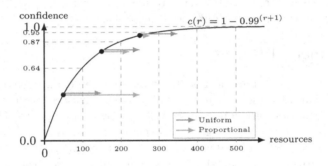

Fig. 4. Allocation of test budget according to common strategies

5.1   RQ1: Theoretical Evaluation

Naive approaches might coincidentally be equally good as elaborate techniques, given the right system architecture and initial confidences. We therefore chose to perform our comparison on a set of randomly generated initial confidences (later referred to as starting points (SPs)) and fault trees (FTs). It is natural to expect `Astrahl`'s insight into system structure and component confidences to outperform naive strategies as the systems grow in size and complexity[3]. Therefore, we only verify `Astrahl`'s superiority on relatively small systems and simple confidence functions. We thus fixed an FT size of six devices connected by five binary `AND` and `OR` gates. Furthermore, confidences behave according to

---

[3] Functional optimisation may not be as efficient in larger dimensions, but even a naive estimate should give a better result than completely ignoring system structure.

the function $c(r) = 1 - 0.99^{(r+1)}$ for all devices, where r represents the invested resources and c the confidence, as displayed in Fig. 4.

Using these settings, we generated 200 FTs and instantiated each with 100 random SPs in the range of 100 to 300, corresponding to initial confidences between approximately 0.64 and 0.95. Using this data set we let `Astrahl` and its competitors distribute total budgets of size 1, 10, 50, 100, 250, 500, and 1000.

5.2   RQ2: Empirical Evaluation

To address RQ2 it is necessary to create an evaluation setting that allows the simulated distribution of (hidden) component faults, their (potential) discovery through testing or experimentation effort and subsequent removal, and finally a calculation of the system confidence based on the remaining, undiscovered faults. Our approach is based on the probabilistic creation of fault distributions (FDs), i.e. assignments of faults to components according to their respective confidences. These faults will be probabilistically found and removed by allocating resources to a component, simulating e.g. experimentation or testing. Our hypothesis is that, given initial component confidences that reflect the components' reliabilities, `Astrahl` should be able to outperform its competitor algorithms and on average lead to higher overall system confidence.

The evaluation process is split into three phases. First, faults are assigned to components according to geometric distributions with parameter $p = 1-c$, where c is our initial confidence in the component. Therefore, components in which we have more confidence will on average contain fewer faults. Next, the faults are removed probabilistically during a "testing phase" as follows. We arbitrarily assume that each test costs 10 resources[4]. Each fault has an observability of 0.1, i.e. each test has a 10% chance to detect this particular fault. When a TRA strategy assigns r resources to a component with n faults, $t = \lfloor \frac{r}{10} \rfloor$ full tests are run on it. Each test has a 10% chance to find and remove each of a component's n faults. If $r > 10t$, i.e. there is remaining budget, a "partial" test is run with proportionally reduced chance to find faults. After this phase, we end up with n' faults in each component. Finally, the system fault probability is calculated. As above, during operation each fault's observability is 0.1, so a component's failure probability can be calculated as $1 - 0.9^{n'}$ if it contains n' faults. The entire system's failure probability can then be calculated using all components' failure probabilities and the standard propagation of fault probabilities in FTs.

Due to the probabilistic nature of this evaluation we repeated this process for 50 FTs, 50 SPs (range 10 to 70)[5] for each FT and 50 random FDs for each SP, totalling to 125,000 FDs. We computed test resource allocations using test budgets of 60, 120, 240, 360, 480 and 600, executed the testing and fault removal process 100 times for each FD and test budget, and subsequently calculated the average FT failure probability, for a total of 75,000,000 computations.

---

[4] It would equally be possible to assume a test costs one resource and scale the budget.

[5] We used smaller confidence so that components will usually contain faults.

5.3   Evaluation Results

The experiment results for RQ1 are shown in Fig. 5a and Fig. 5b. Figure 5a shows the average system reliability according to the total budget and relative difference to Astrahl's score $\frac{(1-r)-(1-r')}{1-r} = \frac{r'-r}{1-r}$, where r is the reliability computed by Astrahl, and r' that computed by its competitor (this measure is closer to intuition than $(r - r')/r$ when both confidences are close 1). The error bars in Fig. 5b represent mean squared error in system reliability. Note that Astrahl outperforms each of the competitors independent of the budget size. It is also noteworthy that although with higher budgets the system becomes very reliable independent of the strategy, the relative performance increase of Astrahl when compared to its competitors grows significantly. In other words, spending a large amount of resources increases obviously the system performance, but it is still better to follow Astrahl's suggestions.

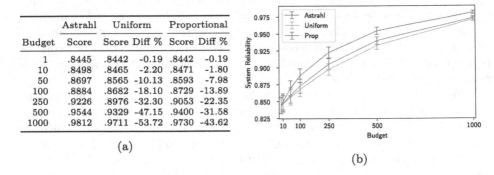

	Astrahl	Uniform		Proportional	
Budget	Score	Score	Diff %	Score	Diff %
1	.8445	.8442	-0.19	.8442	-0.19
10	.8498	.8465	-2.20	.8471	-1.80
50	.8697	.8565	-10.13	.8593	-7.98
100	.8884	.8682	-18.10	.8729	-13.89
250	.9226	.8976	-32.30	.9053	-22.35
500	.9544	.9329	-47.15	.9400	-31.58
1000	.9812	.9711	-53.72	.9730	-43.62

(a)

(b)

Fig. 5. Theoretical evaluation: average system reliability and relative difference

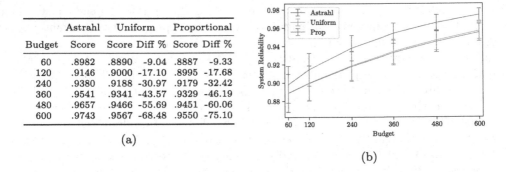

	Astrahl	Uniform		Proportional	
Budget	Score	Score	Diff %	Score	Diff %
60	.8982	.8890	-9.04	.8887	-9.33
120	.9146	.9000	-17.10	.8995	-17.68
240	.9380	.9188	-30.97	.9179	-32.42
360	.9541	.9341	-43.57	.9329	-46.19
480	.9657	.9466	-55.69	.9451	-60.06
600	.9743	.9567	-68.48	.9550	-75.10

(a)

(b)

Fig. 6. Empirical evaluation: system reliability and relative difference

Figure 6a and Fig. 6b display the results of the empirical evaluation (RQ2). Here, the error bars correspond to mean squared error of the average over all

FDs (for each SP). As can be seen, also here `Astrahl` outperforms other TRA strategies. Interestingly though, `Astrahl`'s relative advantage is not as high. An initial investigation suggests the cause for this observation at the discrete nature of the evaluation setting, where in many cases all faults of a component are removed, which leads to full confidence in this component.

Summarising our evaluations it can be said that `Astrahl` is better-suited for identifying where to place test effort than alternative approaches. The experiments show significant relative gains in both theoretical and practical approaches, even for rather small, straightforward systems as in our setting. For more complex systems, we expect `Astrahl`'s insight into the system's structure and the components' confidence should make its advantage even clearer, although this has yet to be validated by experimental results.

6 Conclusion and Future Work

We have defined *Quantitative Confidence Logic*, which represents confidence in assertions and have argued that this logic can help us take system architecture into account when solving the test resource allocation problem (TRAP) and shown the validity of the approach through experimental results. We have also argued that this approach is widely applicable, e. g., because it does not rely on particular assumptions about fault distributions.

The simplicity and versatility of our approach makes it possible to tackle different problems with the same ingredients. An obvious possible future work is to study the TRAP in different settings, for example by implementing multi-objective optimisation, or by studying it in a broader setting, where the confidence gained by running a test depends on the result of the test. We should also experimentally validate our expectation on the scalability of our approach in industry-scale case studies. It would also be interesting to see how solving the TRAP when optimising the total confidence $t + f$ compares to solving it with the current setting, especially on volatile systems. Another possible direction is to study how this approach can be used to solve test prioritisation between different components of a system.

We also want to investigate the logic itself more thouroughly from a purely logical point of view. For example, by changing the interpretation of connectives in three-valued logic, or using different T-norms and T-conorms in the definitions of the rules. Another interesting aspect would be to investigate its links with fuzzy logics and Dempster-Shafer theory deeper, as there seems to be some deep connections. In particular, ties to fuzzy logics would give a bridge between a logic about confidence and a logic about truth, which could help us develop QCL further.

References

1. Bergmann, M.: An Introduction to Many-Valued and Fuzzy Logic: Semantics, Algebras, and Derivation Systems. Cambridge University Press, Cambridge (2008). https://doi.org/10.1017/CBO9780511801129

2. Bertsekas, D.P.: Constrained Optimization and Lagrange Multiplier Methods. Academic Press, Cambridge (2014)
3. Carrozza, G., Pietrantuono, R., Russo, S.: Dynamic test planning: a study in an industrial context. Int. J. Softw. Tools Technol. Transfer **16**(5), 593–607 (2014). https://doi.org/10.1007/s10009-014-0319-0
4. Dempster, A.P.: Upper and lower probabilities induced by a multivalued mapping. Ann. Math. Stat. **36**, 325–339 (1967). https://doi.org/10.1007/978-3-540-44792-4_3
5. Ericson, C.A.: Fault tree analysis. In: System Safety Conference, Orlando, Florida, vol. 1, pp. 1–9 (1999)
6. Esteva, F., Godo, L.: Monoidal T-norm based logic: towards a logic for left-continuous T-norms. Fuzzy Sets Syst. **124**(3), 271–288 (2001). https://doi.org/10.1016/S0165-0114(01)00098-7
7. Goel, A.L., Okumoto, K.: Time-dependent error-detection rate model for software reliability and other performance measures. IEEE Trans. Reliab. **28**(3), 206–211 (1979). https://doi.org/10.1109/TR.1979.5220566
8. Hájek, P.: Metamathematics of Fuzzy Logic, vol. 4. Springer Science & Business Media, Dordrecht (2013). https://doi.org/10.1007/978-94-011-5300-3
9. Hansen, N., Ostermeier, A.: Completely derandomized self-adaptation in evolution strategies. Evol. Comput. **9**(2), 159–195 (2001). https://doi.org/10.1162/106365601750190398
10. Huang, C.Y., Lo, J.H.: Optimal resource allocation for cost and reliability of modular software systems in the testing phase. J. Syst. Softw. **79**(5), 653–664 (2006). https://doi.org/10.1016/j.jss.2005.06.039
11. Kamei, Y., Shihab, E.: Defect Prediction: Accomplishments and Future Challenges. In: 2016 IEEE 23rd International Conference on Software Analysis, Evolution, and Reengineering (SANER), vol. 5, pp. 33–45. IEEE (2016). https://doi.org/10.1109/SANER.2016.56
12. Pietrantuono, R.: On the testing resource allocation problem: research trends and perspectives. J. Syst. Softw. **161**, 110462 (2020). https://doi.org/10.1016/j.jss.2019.110462
13. Pietrantuono, R., Russo, S., Trivedi, K.S.: Software reliability and testing time allocation: an architecture-based approach. IEEE Trans. Softw. Eng. **36**(3), 323–337 (2010). https://doi.org/10.1109/TSE.2010.6
14. Sallak, M., Schön, W., Aguirre, F.: Reliability assessment for multi-state systems under uncertainties based on the Dempster-Shafer theory. IIE Trans. **45**(9), 995–1007 (2013). https://doi.org/10.1080/0740817X.2012.706378
15. Shafer, G.: A Mathematical Theory of Evidence, vol. 42. Princeton University Press, Princeton (1976). https://doi.org/10.2307/j.ctv10vm1qb
16. Van Laarhoven, P.J., Aarts, E.H.: Simulated annealing. In: Simulated Annealing: Theory and Applications. MAIA, vol. 37, pp. 7–15. Springer, Dordrecht (1987). https://doi.org/10.1007/978-94-015-7744-1_2
17. Vesely, W.E., Goldberg, F.F., Roberts, N.H., Haasl, D.F.: Fault Tree Handbook. Technical Report, Nuclear Regulatory Commission Washington DC (1981)
18. Yamada, S., Osaki, S.: Software reliability growth modeling: models and applications. IEEE Trans. Softw. Eng. **SE-11**(12), 1431–1437 (1985). https://doi.org/10.1109/TSE.1985.232179
19. Zhang, G., Su, Z., Li, M., Yue, F., Jiang, J., Yao, X.: Constraint handling in NSGA-II for solving optimal testing resource allocation problems. IEEE Trans. Reliab. **66**(4), 1193–1212 (2017). https://doi.org/10.1109/TR.2017.2738660

A Benchmarks Library for Extended Parametric Timed Automata

Étienne André[1] , Dylan Marinho[1(✉)] ,
and Jaco van de Pol[2]

[1] Université de Lorraine, CNRS, Inria, LORIA, 54000 Nancy, France
`dylan.marinho@loria.fr`
[2] Department of Computer Science, Aarhus University, Aarhus, Denmark

Abstract. Parametric timed automata are a powerful formalism for reasoning on concurrent real-time systems with unknown or uncertain timing constants. In order to test the efficiency of new algorithms, a fair set of benchmarks is required. We present an extension of the IMITATOR benchmarks library, that accumulated over the years a number of case studies from academic and industrial contexts. We extend here the library with several dozens of new benchmarks; these benchmarks highlight several new features: liveness properties, extensions of (parametric) timed automata (including stopwatches or multi-rate clocks), and unsolvable toy benchmarks. These latter additions help to emphasize the limits of state-of-the-art parameter synthesis techniques, with the hope to develop new dedicated algorithms in the future.

Keywords: Case studies · Models · Parametric timed automata

1 Introduction

Timed automata (TAs) [10] are a powerful formalism for reasoning on concurrent real-time systems. Their parametric extension (*parametric timed automata*, PTAs [11]) offer the use of *timing parameters* (unknown or uncertain timing constants), allowing to verify properties on a model at an earlier design stage, or when the exact values of constants at runtime may be unknown. The model checking problem with its binary answer ("yes"/"no") becomes the *parameter synthesis* problem: "for which values of the parameters does the model satisfy its specification?".

In the past few years, a growing number of new synthesis algorithms were proposed for PTAs, e.g., using bounded model-checking [38], compositional verification [24,26], distributed verification [20], for liveness properties [18,27,43], for dedicated problems [31]—notably for testing timed systems [14,17,18,34,41,42]. However, these works consider different benchmarks sets, making it difficult to evaluate which technique is the most efficient for each application domain.

This work is partially supported by the ANR-NRF French-Singaporean research program ProMiS (ANR-19-CE25-0015).

F. Loulergue and F. Wotawa (Eds.): TAP 2021, LNCS 12740, pp. 39–50, 2021.
https://doi.org/10.1007/978-3-030-79379-1_3

A benchmarks suite for (extended) PTAs can be used for different purposes: *i)* when developing new algorithms for (extensions of) PTAs and testing their efficiency by comparing them with existing techniques; *ii)* when evaluating benchmarks for extensions of TAs [10] (note that valuating our benchmarks with a parameter valuation yields a timed or multi-rate automaton); and *iii)* when looking for benchmarks fitting in the larger class of *hybrid* automata [9].

Contribution. In [2,15], we introduced a first library of 34 benchmarks and 122 properties, for PTAs. However, this former library suffers from several issues. First, its syntax is only compatible with the syntax of version 2.12 of IMITATOR [21], while IMITATOR recently shifted to version 3.0 [16], with a different calling paradigm.[1] Second, the former version contains exclusively safety/reachability properties (plus some "robustness" computations [23]). Third, only syntactic information is provided (benchmarks, metrics on the benchmarks), and no semantic information (expected result, approximate computation time, and number of states to explore).

In this work, we extend our former library with a list of new features, including syntactic extensions (notably multi-rate clocks [8]); we also focus on *unsolvable* case studies, i.e., simple examples for which no known algorithm allows computation of the result, with the ultimate goal to encourage the community to address these cases. In addition, we add *liveness* properties. Also, we add *semantic* criteria, with an approximate computation time for the properties, an expected result (whenever available) and an approximate number of explored states. The rationale is to help users by giving them an idea of what to expect for each case study. Also, our consolidated classification aims at helping tool developers to select within our library which benchmarks suit them (e.g., "PTAs without stopwatches, with many locations and a large state space").

To summarize, we propose a new version of our library enhancing the former one as follows:

1. adding 22 new benchmarks (39 models)
   - adding benchmarks for *liveness* properties;
   - adding a set of toy *unsolvable* benchmarks, to emphasize the limits of state-of-the-art parametric verification techniques, and to encourage the community to develop new dedicated algorithms in the future;
2. refactoring all existing benchmarks, so that they now implement the syntax of the 3.0 version of IMITATOR;
3. providing a better classification of benchmarks;
4. highlighting extensions of (parametric) timed automata, such as multi-rate clocks [8], stopwatches [29], . . .
5. offering an automated translation of our benchmarks to the new JANI [1, 28] model interchange format, offering a unified format for quantitative

---

[1] While many keywords remain the same in the model, the property syntax has been completely rewritten, and the model checker now takes as input a model file *and* a property file. In addition, new properties are now possible, and the syntax has been extended with some useful features such as multi-rate clocks.

automata-based formalisms. This way, the library can be used by any tool using JANI as an input format, and supporting (extensions of) TAs. Even though other tools implementing the JANI formalism do not handle parameters, they can run on *instances* of our benchmarks, i.e., by valuating the PTAs with concrete valuations of the parameters.

Table 1. Selected new features

Library	Size			Metrics		Format		Categories	Properties			Analysis
Version	Bench.	Models	Prop.	Static	Semantic	.imi	JANI	Unsolvable	EF	TPS	liveness	Results
1.0 [2]	34	80	122	√	×	2.12	×	×	√	√	×	×
2.0 [6]	56	119	216	√	√	3.0	√	√	√	√	√	√

We summarize the most significant dimensions of our extension in Table 1. EF (using the TCTL syntax) denotes reachability/safety, and TPS ("trace preservation synthesis") denotes robustness analysis.

Outline. We discuss related libraries in Sect. 2. We briefly recall IMITATOR PTAs in Sect. 3. We present our library in Sect. 4, and we give perspectives in Sect. 5.

2   Related Libraries

RTLib [45] is a library of real-time systems modeled as timed automata. Contrary to our solution, it does not consider parametric models.

Two hybrid systems benchmarks libraries were proposed in [30,32]. Despite being more expressive than PTAs in theory, these formalisms cannot be compared in practice: most of them do not refer to timing parameters. Moreover, these libraries only focus on reachability properties.

The PRISM benchmark suite [39] collects probabilistic models and properties. Despite including some timing aspects, time is not the focus there.

The collection of Matlab/Simulink models [36] focuses on timed model checking, but has no parametric extensions. Two of our benchmarks (`accel` and `gear`) originate from a translation of their models to (extensions of) PTAs [22].

The JANI specification [28] defines a representation of automata with quantitative extensions and variables. A library of JANI benchmarks is also provided; such benchmarks come from PRISM, Modest, Storm and FIG, and therefore cannot be applied to parameter synthesis for timed systems.

Also, a number of model checking competitions started in the last two decades, accumulating over the years a number of sets of benchmarks, such as the ARCH "friendly competition" [3,33], the Petri Nets model checking contest [5,12], the MARS workshop repository [4], the WATERS workshop series [44], etc.

Our library aims at providing benchmarks for *parameter* synthesis for (extensions of) TAs. Notably, we go beyond the TA syntax (offering some benchmarks with multi-rate clocks, stopwatches, timing parameters, additional global variables), while not offering the full power of hybrid automata (differential equations, complex flows). To the best of our knowledge, no other set of benchmarks addresses specifically the *synthesis* of timing parameters.

3   Parametric Timed Automata

Parametric Timed Automata (PTAs). Timed automata (TAs) [10] extend finite-state automata with *clocks*, i.e., real-valued variables evolving at the same rate 1, that can be compared to integers along edges ("guards") or within locations ("invariants"). Clocks can be reset (to 0) along transitions. PTAs extend TAs with (timing) parameters, i.e., unknown rational-valued constants [11]. These timing parameters can have two main purposes:

- model unknown constants, and *synthesize* suitable values for them, at an early design stage; or
- verify the system for a full range of constants, as their actual value may not be exactly known before execution; this is notably the case of the FMTV Challenge by Thales at WATERS 2015 [44] that features periods known with a limited precision only (i.e., constant but of unknown exact value), and that we were able to solve using parametric timed automata [46]. (This benchmark FMTV1 is part of our library.)

PTAs can be synchronized together on shared actions, or by reading shared variables. That is, it is possible to perform the parallel composition of several PTAs, using a common actions alphabet. This allows users to define models component by component.

Example 1. Consider the toy PTA in Fig. 2a. It features two clocks x and y, one parameter p and two locations. ℓ_0 is the initial location, while ℓ_f is accepting. The *invariant*, defining the condition to be fulfilled to remain in a location, is depicted as a dotted box below the location (e.g., $x \leq 1$ in ℓ_0). A transition from ℓ_0 to ℓ_f can be taken when its *guard* ("$x = 0 \wedge y = p$") is satisfied; the other transition (looping on ℓ_0) can be taken whenever $x = 1$, resetting x to 0.

Observe that, if $p = 0$, then the guard $x = 0 \wedge y = 0$ is immediately true, and ℓ_f is reachable in 0-time. If $p = 1$, the guard becomes $x = 0 \wedge y = 1$, which is not initially satisfied, and one needs to loop once over ℓ_0, yielding $x = 0 \wedge y = 1$, after which ℓ_f is reachable. In fact, it can be shown that the answer to the reachability synthesis problem "synthesize the valuations of p such that ℓ_f is reachable" is exactly $p = i, i \in \mathbb{N}$.

Extending the PTAs Syntax. Our library follows the IMITATOR syntax. Therefore, some benchmarks (clearly marked as such) go beyond the traditional PTAs syntax, and are referred to IPTAs (IMITATOR PTAs). These extensions include:

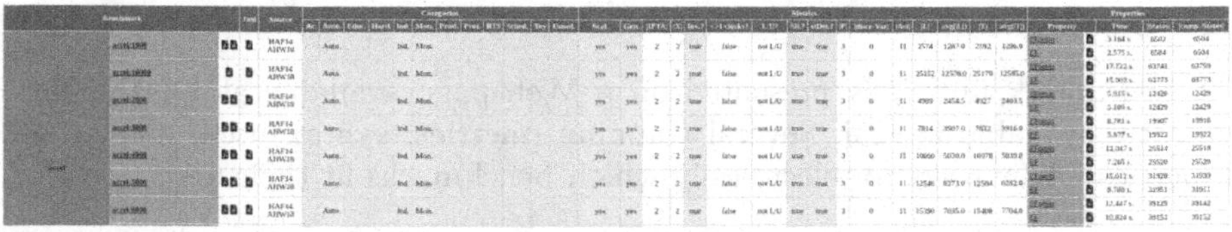

Fig. 1. The IMITATOR benchmark library Web page

Urgent locations. Locations where time cannot elapse.

Global rational-valued variables. Such "discrete" variables can be updated along transitions, and can also be part of the clock guards and invariants.

Arbitrary flows. Some benchmarks require arbitrary (constant) flows for clocks; this way, clocks do not necessary evolve at the same time, and can encode different concepts from only time, e.g., temperature, amount of completion, continuous cost. Their value can increase or decrease at any predefined rate in each location, and can become negative. In that sense, these clocks are closer to *continuous variables* (as in hybrid automata) rather than TAs' clocks; nevertheless, they still have a constant flow, while hybrid automata can have more general flows. This makes some of our benchmarks fit into a parametric extension of *multi-rate automata* [8]. This notably includes stopwatches, where clocks can have a 1 or 0-rate [29].

4 The Benchmarks Library

4.1 Organization

The library is made of a set of *benchmarks*. Each benchmark may have different *models*: for example, Gear comes with ten models, of different sizes (the number of locations notably varies), named Gear:1000 to Gear:10000. Similarly, some Fischer benchmarks come with several models, each of them corresponding to a different number of processes. Finally, each model comes with one or more *properties*. For example, for Gear:2000, one can run either reachability synthesis, or minimal reachability synthesis.

The benchmark library, in its 2.0 version, covers 56 benchmarks, which group 119 models and 216 properties.

From the previous version [15], 39 models have been added: beyond all Unsolvable models, and a few more additions, we notably added a second model of the Bounded Retransmission Protocol (BRPAAPP21), recently proposed in [18].

Benchmarks come from industrial collaborations (e.g., with Thales, ST-Microelectronics, ArianeGroup, Astrium), from academic papers from different communities (e.g., real-time systems, monitoring, testing) describing case studies, and from our experience in the field (notably the "unsolvable" benchmarks). For benchmarks extracted from published works, a complete bibliographic reference is given.

4.2 Distribution

The benchmark library is presented on a Web page available at [6] and permanently available at [25]. Several columns (metrics, syntax used, categories, properties) allow users to select easily which benchmarks fit their need (see Fig. 1).

Our benchmarks are distributed in the well-documented IMITATOR 3.0.0 input format [16], which is a *de facto* standard for PTAs. IMITATOR can provide automated translations to the non-parametric timed model checker UPPAAL [40], as well as the hybrid systems model checker HYTECH [35] (not maintained anymore). However, some differences (presence of timing parameters or complex guards in IMITATOR, difference in the semantics of the synchronization model) may not preserve the semantic equivalence of the models.

In addition, we offer all benchmarks in the JANI format [28]. We recently implemented to this end (within IMITATOR) an automatic translation of IPTAs to their JANI specification. Thus, all of our benchmarks can be fed to other verification tools supporting JANI as input.

All our benchmarks are released under the CC by 4.0 license.

4.3 Benchmarks Classification

For each benchmark, we provide multiple criteria, notably the following ones.

Scalability. Whether the models can be scaled according to some metrics, e.g., the FischerPS08 benchmark can be scaled according to the number of processes competing for the critical section;

Generation method. Whether the models are automatically generated or not (e.g., by a script, notably for scheduling real-time systems using PTAs, or to generate random words in benchmarks from the testing or monitoring communities);

Categorization. Benchmarks are tagged with one or more categories: 1) Academic, 2) Automotive, 3) Education, 4) Hardware, 5) Industrial, 6) Monitoring, 7) Producer-consumer, 8) Protocol, 9) Real-time system, 10) Scheduling, 11) Toy, 12) Unsolvable. The proportion of each of these tags are given in Table 2 (the sum exceeds 100 % since benchmarks can belong to multiple categories).

Moreover, we use the following static metrics to categorize our benchmarks: 1) the numbers of PTA components (subject to parallel composition), of clocks, parameters, discrete variables and actions; 2) whether the benchmark has invariants, whether some clocks have a rate not equal to 1 (multi-rate/stopwatch) and silent actions ("ϵ-transitions"); 3) whether the benchmark is an L/U-PTA[2]; 5) the numbers of locations and transitions, and the total number of transitions.

In Table 3, we present some statistics on our benchmarks. Because of the presence of 3 benchmarks and 25 models (all in the "monitoring" category) with

---

[2] A subclass of PTAs where the set of parameters is partitioned into "lower-bound" and "upper-bound" parameters [37]. L/U-PTAs enjoy nicer decidability properties.

Table 2. Proportion of each category over the models

Category	Number of models	Proportion
All	119	100 %
Academic	54	45 %
Automotive	20	17 %
Education	9	8 %
Hardware	6	5 %
Industrial	33	28 %
Monitoring	25	21 %
ProdCons	5	4 %
Protocol	34	29 %
RTS	46	39 %
Scheduling	3	3 %
Toy	34	29 %
Unsolvable	18	15 %

Table 3. Statistics on the benchmarks

Metric	Average	Median
Number of IPTAs	3	3
Number of clocks	4	3
Number of parameters	4	3
Number of discrete variables	4	2
Number of actions	12	11
Total number of locations	2004	22
Total number of transitions	2280	54

Metric	Percentage
Has invariants?	92 %
Has discrete variables?	24 %
Has multi-rate clocks	17 %
L/U subclass	19 %
Has silent actions?	67 %
Strongly deterministic?	78 %

a very large number of locations (up to several dozens of thousands), only giving the average of some metrics is irrelevant. To this end, we also provide the *median* values. Moreover, the average and the median of the number of discrete variables are computed only on the benchmarks which contains at least 1 such variable; they represent 24% of our models.

4.4 Properties

Properties follow the IMITATOR syntax. In the 1.0 version, they mainly consisted of reachability/safety properties; in addition, the properties were not explicitly provided, since IMITATOR 2.x did not specify properties (they were provided using options in the executed command). In the new version of our library, we added several *liveness* (cycle synthesis) properties, i.e., for which one aims at synthesizing parameter valuations featuring at least one infinite (accepting) run [18,43]; in addition, we added properties such as deadlock-freeness

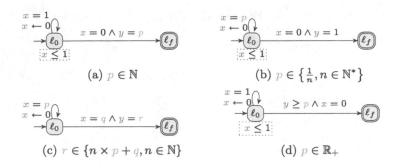

Fig. 2. Examples of unsolvable benchmarks

Table 4. Statistics on executions (over 157 properties)

Metric	Average	Median
Total computation time	245.8	2.819
Number of states	20817.8	580
Number of computed states	34571.7	1089

synthesis ("exhibit parameter valuations for which the model is deadlock-free") [14], optimal-parameter or minimal-time reachability [19], and some "pattern"-based properties [13] that eventually reduce to reachability checking [7].

4.5   Unsolvable Benchmarks

A novelty of our library is to provide a set of toy unsolvable benchmarks. They have been chosen for being beyond the limits of the state-of-the-art techniques. Four of them are illustrated in Fig. 2. For example, in Fig. 2a, the reachability of ℓ_f is achievable only if $p \in \mathbb{N}$; but no verification tool—to the best of our knowledge—terminates this computation. Moreover, the final location of the PTA presented in Fig. 2d is reachable for all $p \geq 0$, which is a convex constraint, but this solution remains not computable.

4.6   Expected Performances

Another novelty of the 2.0 version is to provide users with all the expected results, as generated by IMITATOR. For all properties, we provide either a computed result, or (for the "unsolvable" benchmarks), a human-solved theoretical result.

We also give an approximate execution time, and the number of (symbolic) states explored. These metrics are not strict, as they may depend on the target model checker and the target hardware/OS, but this provides the user an idea of the complexity of our models.

In Table 4, we present the statistics over 157 imitator executions. Note that the *unsolvable* executions are not included in this table.

5   Perspectives

Ultimately, we hope our library can serve as a basis for a *parametric* timed model checking competition, a concept yet missing in the model checking community.
    Opening the library to volunteer contributions is also on our agenda.

Acknowledgements. Experiments presented in this paper were carried out using the Grid'5000 testbed, supported by a scientific interest group hosted by Inria and including CNRS, RENATER and several Universities as well as other organizations (see https://www.grid5000.fr).

References

1. JANI specification (2017). https://jani-spec.org/
2. The IMITATOR benchmarks library v1.0 (2018). https://www.imitator.fr/library1.html
3. ARCH benchmarks (2021). https://cps-vo.org/group/ARCH/benchmarks
4. MARS repository (2021). http://www.mars-workshop.org/repository.html
5. Model checking contest (2021). https://mcc.lip6.fr/
6. The IMITATOR benchmarks library v2.0 (2021). https://www.imitator.fr/static/library2/
7. Aceto, L., Bouyer, P., Burgueño, A., Larsen, K.G.: The power of reachability testing for timed automata. TCS **300**(1–3), 411–475 (2003). https://doi.org/10.1016/S0304-3975(02)00334-1
8. Alur, R., et al.: The algorithmic analysis of hybrid systems. TCS **138**(1), 3–34 (1995). https://doi.org/10.1016/0304-3975(94)00202-T
9. Alur, R., Courcoubetis, C., Henzinger, T.A., Ho, P.-H.: Hybrid automata: an algorithmic approach to the specification and verification of hybrid systems. In: Grossman, R.L., Nerode, A., Ravn, A.P., Rischel, H. (eds.) HS 1991-1992. LNCS, vol. 736, pp. 209–229. Springer, Heidelberg (1993). https://doi.org/10.1007/3-540-57318-6_30
10. Alur, R., Dill, D.L.: A theory of timed automata. TCS **126**(2), 183–235 (1994). https://doi.org/10.1016/0304-3975(94)90010-8
11. Alur, R., Henzinger, T.A., Vardi, M.Y.: Parametric real-time reasoning. In: Kosaraju, S.R., Johnson, D.S., Aggarwal, A. (eds.) STOC, pp. 592–601. ACM, New York (1993). https://doi.org/10.1145/167088.167242
12. Amparore, E., et al.: Presentation of the 9th edition of the model checking contest. In: Beyer, D., Huisman, M., Kordon, F., Steffen, B. (eds.) TACAS 2019. LNCS, vol. 11429, pp. 50–68. Springer, Cham (2019). https://doi.org/10.1007/978-3-030-17502-3_4
13. André, É.: Observer patterns for real-time systems. In: Liu, Y., Martin, A. (eds.) ICECCS, pp. 125–134. IEEE Computer Society, July 2013. https://doi.org/10.1109/ICECCS.2013.26
14. André, É.: Parametric deadlock-freeness checking timed automata. In: Sampaio, A., Wang, F. (eds.) ICTAC 2016. LNCS, vol. 9965, pp. 469–478. Springer, Cham (2016). https://doi.org/10.1007/978-3-319-46750-4_27
15. André, É.: A benchmark library for parametric timed model checking. In: Artho, C., Ölveczky, P.C. (eds.) FTSCS 2018. CCIS, vol. 1008, pp. 75–83. Springer, Cham (2019). https://doi.org/10.1007/978-3-030-12988-0_5

16. André, É.: IMITATOR user manual (2021). https://github.com/imitator-model-checker/imitator/releases/download/v3.1.0-beta/IMITATOR-user-manual.pdf
17. André, É., Arcaini, P., Gargantini, A., Radavelli, M.: Repairing timed automata clock guards through abstraction and testing. In: Beyer, D., Keller, C. (eds.) TAP 2019. LNCS, vol. 11823, pp. 129–146. Springer, Cham (2019). https://doi.org/10.1007/978-3-030-31157-5_9
18. André, É., Arias, J., Petrucci, L., van de Pol, J.: Iterative bounded synthesis for efficient cycle detection in parametric timed automata. In: Groote, J.F., Larsen, K.G. (eds.) TACAS (2021)
19. André, É., Bloemen, V., Petrucci, L., van de Pol, J.: Minimal-time synthesis for parametric timed automata. In: Vojnar, T., Zhang, L. (eds.) TACAS 2019. LNCS, vol. 11428, pp. 211–228. Springer, Cham (2019). https://doi.org/10.1007/978-3-030-17465-1_12
20. André, É., Coti, C., Nguyen, H.G.: Enhanced distributed behavioral cartography of parametric timed automata. In: Butler, M., Conchon, S., Zaïdi, F. (eds.) ICFEM 2015. LNCS, vol. 9407, pp. 319–335. Springer, Cham (2015). https://doi.org/10.1007/978-3-319-25423-4_21
21. André, É., Fribourg, L., Kühne, U., Soulat, R.: IMITATOR 2.5: a tool for analyzing robustness in scheduling problems. In: Giannakopoulou, D., Méry, D. (eds.) FM 2012. LNCS, vol. 7436, pp. 33–36. Springer, Heidelberg (2012). https://doi.org/10.1007/978-3-642-32759-9_6
22. André, É., Hasuo, I., Waga, M.: Offline timed pattern matching under uncertainty. In: Lin, A.W., Sun, J. (eds.) ICECCS, pp. 10–20. IEEE Computer Society (2018). https://doi.org/10.1109/ICECCS2018.2018.00010
23. André, É., Lime, D., Markey, N.: Language preservation problems in parametric timed automata. LMCS **16**(1) (2020). https://doi.org/10.23638/LMCS-16(1:5)2020. https://lmcs.episciences.org/6042
24. André, É., Lin, S.-W.: Learning-based compositional parameter synthesis for event-recording automata. In: Bouajjani, A., Silva, A. (eds.) FORTE 2017. LNCS, vol. 10321, pp. 17–32. Springer, Cham (2017). https://doi.org/10.1007/978-3-319-60225-7_2
25. André, É., Marinho, D., van de Pol, J.: The IMITATOR benchmarks library 2.0: a benchmarks library for extended parametric timed automata, April 2021. https://doi.org/10.5281/zenodo.4730980
26. Aştefănoaei, L., Bensalem, S., Bozga, M., Cheng, C.-H., Ruess, H.: Compositional parameter synthesis. In: Fitzgerald, J., Heitmeyer, C., Gnesi, S., Philippou, A. (eds.) FM 2016. LNCS, vol. 9995, pp. 60–68. Springer, Cham (2016). https://doi.org/10.1007/978-3-319-48989-6_4
27. Bezděk, P., Beneš, N., Barnat, J., Černá, I.: LTL parameter synthesis of parametric timed automata. In: De Nicola, R., Kühn, E. (eds.) SEFM 2016. LNCS, vol. 9763, pp. 172–187. Springer, Cham (2016). https://doi.org/10.1007/978-3-319-41591-8_12
28. Budde, C.E., Dehnert, C., Hahn, E.M., Hartmanns, A., Junges, S., Turrini, A.: JANI: quantitative model and tool interaction. In: Legay, A., Margaria, T. (eds.) TACAS 2017. LNCS, vol. 10206, pp. 151–168. Springer, Heidelberg (2017). https://doi.org/10.1007/978-3-662-54580-5_9
29. Cassez, F., Larsen, K.: The impressive power of stopwatches. In: Palamidessi, C. (ed.) CONCUR 2000. LNCS, vol. 1877, pp. 138–152. Springer, Heidelberg (2000). https://doi.org/10.1007/3-540-44618-4_12

30. Chen, X., Schupp, S., Makhlouf, I.B., Ábrahám, E., Frehse, G., Kowalewski, S.: A benchmark suite for hybrid systems reachability analysis. In: Havelund, K., Holzmann, G., Joshi, R. (eds.) NFM 2015. LNCS, vol. 9058, pp. 408–414. Springer, Cham (2015). https://doi.org/10.1007/978-3-319-17524-9_29
31. Cimatti, A., Palopoli, L., Ramadian, Y.: Symbolic computation of schedulability regions using parametric timed automata. In: RTSS, pp. 80–89. IEEE Computer Society (2008). https://doi.org/10.1109/RTSS.2008.36
32. Fehnker, A., Ivančić, F.: Benchmarks for hybrid systems verification. In: Alur, R., Pappas, G.J. (eds.) HSCC 2004. LNCS, vol. 2993, pp. 326–341. Springer, Heidelberg (2004). https://doi.org/10.1007/978-3-540-24743-2_22
33. Frehse, G., et al.: ARCH-COMP19 category report: hybrid systems with piecewise constant dynamics. In: ARCH@CPSIoTWeek. EPiC Series in Computing, vol. 61, pp. 1–13. EasyChair (2019)
34. Fribourg, L., Kühne, U.: Parametric verification and test coverage for hybrid automata using the inverse method. Int. J. Found. Comput. Sci. 24(2), 233–249 (2013). https://doi.org/10.1142/S0129054113400091
35. Henzinger, T.A., Ho, P.-H., Wong-Toi, H.: A user guide to HyTech. In: Brinksma, E., Cleaveland, W.R., Larsen, K.G., Margaria, T., Steffen, B. (eds.) TACAS 1995. LNCS, vol. 1019, pp. 41–71. Springer, Heidelberg (1995). https://doi.org/10.1007/3-540-60630-0_3
36. Hoxha, B., Abbas, H., Fainekos, G.E.: Benchmarks for temporal logic requirements for automotive systems. In: Frehse, G., Althoff, M. (eds.) ARCH@CPSWeek. EPiC Series in Computing, vol. 34, pp. 25–30. EasyChair (2014). http://www.easychair.org/publications/paper/250954
37. Hune, T., Romijn, J., Stoelinga, M., Vaandrager, F.W.: Linear parametric model checking of timed automata. JLAP 52–53, 183–220 (2002). https://doi.org/10.1016/S1567-8326(02)00037-1
38. Knapik, M., Penczek, W.: Bounded model checking for parametric timed automata. Trans. Petri Nets Other Models Concurrency 5, 141–159 (2012). https://doi.org/10.1007/978-3-642-29072-5_6
39. Kwiatkowska, M.Z., Norman, G., Parker, D.: The PRISM benchmark suite. In: Ninth International Conference on Quantitative Evaluation of Systems, QEST 2012, London, United Kingdom, 17–20 September 2012, pp. 203–204. IEEE Computer Society (2012). https://doi.org/10.1109/QEST.2012.14
40. Larsen, K.G., Pettersson, P., Yi, W.: UPPAAL in a nutshell. STTT 1(1–2), 134–152 (1997). https://doi.org/10.1007/s100090050010
41. Luthmann, L., Gerecht, T., Stephan, A., Bürdek, J., Lochau, M.: Minimum/maximum delay testing of product lines with unbounded parametric real-time constraints. J. Syst. Softw. 149, 535–553 (2019). https://doi.org/10.1016/j.jss.2018.12.028
42. Luthmann, L., Stephan, A., Bürdek, J., Lochau, M.: Modeling and testing product lines with unbounded parametric real-time constraints. In: Cohen, M.B., et al. (eds.) SPLC, Volume A, pp. 104–113. ACM (2017). https://doi.org/10.1145/3106195.3106204
43. Nguyen, H.G., Petrucci, L., van de Pol, J.: Layered and collecting NDFS with subsumption for parametric timed automata. In: Lin, A.W., Sun, J. (eds.) ICECCS, pp. 1–9. IEEE Computer Society, December 2018. https://doi.org/10.1109/ICECCS2018.2018.00009
44. Quinton, S., Vardanega, T.: 6th International Workshop on Analysis Tools and Methodologies for Embedded and Real-Time Systems (WATERS). http://waters2015.inria.fr/

45. Shan, L., Graf, S., Quinton, S.: RTLib: A Library of Timed Automata for Modeling Real-Time Systems. Research report, Grenoble 1 UGA - Université Grenoble Alpe; INRIA Grenoble - Rhone-Alpes, November 2016. https://hal.archives-ouvertes.fr/hal-01393888
46. Sun, Y., André, É., Lipari, G.: Verification of two real-time systems using parametric timed automata. In: Quinton, S., Vardanega, T. (eds.) WATERS, July 2015

Testing

Generating Timed UI Tests from Counterexamples

Dominik Diner, Gordon Fraser$^{(\boxtimes)}$, Sebastian Schweikl,
and Andreas Stahlbauer

University of Passau, Passau, Germany
gordon.fraser@uni-passau.de

Abstract. One of the largest communities on learning programming
and sharing code is built around the SCRATCH programming language,
which fosters visual and block-based programming. An essential requirement for building learning environments that support learners and educators is automated program analysis. Although the code written by
learners is often simple, analyzing this code to show its correctness or
to provide support is challenging, since SCRATCH programs are graphical, game-like programs that are controlled by the user using mouse
and keyboard. While model checking offers an effective means to analyze
such programs, the output of a model checker is difficult to interpret for
users, in particular for novices. In this work, we introduce the notion of
SCRATCH error witnesses that help to explain the presence of a specification violation. SCRATCH error witnesses describe sequences of timed
inputs to SCRATCH programs leading to a program state that violates
the specification. We present an approach for automatically extracting
error witnesses from counterexamples produced by a model checking procedure. The resulting error witnesses can be exchanged with a testing
framework, where they can be automatically re-played in order to reproduce the specification violations. Error witnesses can not only aid the
user in understanding the misbehavior of a program, but can also enable
the interaction between different verification tools, and therefore open
up new possibilities for the combination of static and dynamic analysis.

Keywords: Error witnesses · Model checking · Reachability · Dynamic
analysis · Test generation · Block-based programming · UI testing

1 Introduction

Block-based programming languages like SCRATCH have gained momentum as
part of the general trend to integrate programming into general education. Their
widespread use will crucially depend on automated program analysis to enable
learning environments in which learners and educators receive the necessary help
for assessing progress, finding errors, and receiving feedback or hints on how to
proceed with a problem at hand. Although learners' programs tend to be small

© Springer Nature Switzerland AG 2021
F. Loulergue and F. Wotawa (Eds.): TAP 2021, LNCS 12740, pp. 53–71, 2021.
https://doi.org/10.1007/978-3-030-79379-1_4

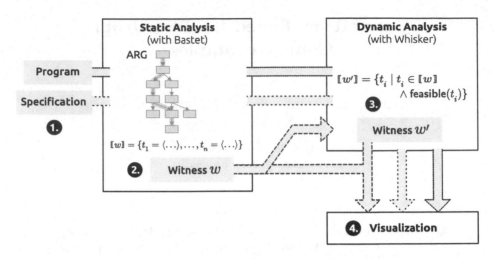

Fig. 1. Generation, verification, and visualization of SCRATCH error witnesses

and their code is usually not very complex, SCRATCH programs nevertheless pose unique challenges for program analysis tools: they are highly concurrent, graphical, driven by user interactions, typically game-like and nondeterministic, and story-components and animations often lead to very long execution times. Model checking has been suggested as a solution for tackling these challenges [19], but verification results such as counterexamples are abstract and neither suitable for interpretation by learners, nor for application in dynamic analysis tools that aim to generate explanations or hints.

Observing program executions in terms of the user interactions and their graphical responses is potentially a more intuitive way to communicate counterexamples to learners, as it hides all details of the internal models of the analysis and verification tool and instead shows what a user would see. In this paper we therefore introduce the concept of SCRATCH *error witnesses* as a means to explain the presence of specification violations, and describe an automatic approach for extracting error witnesses for SCRATCH programs from counterexamples. SCRATCH error witnesses describe sequences of timed inputs (e.g., mouse and keyboard inputs) to SCRATCH programs leading to a program state that violates the specification. Error witnesses are, essentially, UI tests, and thus enable any form of dynamic analysis to help produce more elaborate explanations or feedback, such as fault localization or generation of fix suggestions.

Figure 1 provides an overview of the overall process of generating, verifying, and visualizing error witnesses. A SCRATCH program and its formal specification is given ❶ to the static analysis tool, in this case to BASTET [19]. To analyze the program, BASTET constructs an abstract reachability graph (ARG), which represents an overapproximation of all possible states and behaviors of the program—a node in this graph is an abstract state, representing a set of concrete program states. When BASTET runs into an abstract state in which the specification is violated, an error witness w is produced. An abstract witness may represent multiple concrete test candidates, and depending on the analysis configuration of BASTET (for example, model checking, or data-flow analysis), some of these may be false positives. To increase confidence in the witness, it is handed over ❷ to a dynamic analysis (in this case WHISKER [20]), which runs the tests that are described by the witness, and produces a new error witness w' ❸, with $[\![w']\!] \subseteq [\![w]\!]$. In case none of the tests in w are feasible, the result is an empty witness, that is, $[\![w']\!] = \emptyset$. With this increased confidence in the presence of a specification violation, the refined witness can be visualized ❹ for the user, without reducing his or her trust in the analysis results. Trust in analysis results is crucial, for example, for learners who are not familiar with program analysis, and for automated grading or feedback approaches.

Error witnesses do not only have the potential to aid the user in understanding the misbehavior of a program, but they can also be exchanged among different verification tools [3]. This makes it possible to take advantage of the complementary strengths of both dynamic and static analyses. For example, one can use dynamic analysis for verifying the witnesses, for applying fault localization to narrow down the origin the failure, for generating fixes and repair suggestions, or for guiding the state-space exploration to reach a particular state. Error witnesses thus lay the foundations for future research on presenting counterexamples for specification violations in SCRATCH programs to users.

2 Preliminaries

We stick to the notation that is used in recent work on formalizing SCRATCH programs [19,20]. Uppercase letters $A, \ldots, Z$ denote *sets*, lowercase letters $a, \ldots, z$ denote set *elements*. *Sequences* are enclosed in angled brackets $\langle a_1, a_2, \ldots \rangle$, *tuples* are enclosed in parentheses $(a_1, b_1, \ldots)$, *sets* are enclosed in curly braces $\{a_1, \ldots\}$. Symbols with an overline $\overline{a}$ denote sequences, lists, or vectors. Symbols with a hat $\hat{a}$ denote sets. Symbols with a tilde $\tilde{a}$ denote relations. The set of all *finite words* over an alphabet A is denoted by A^*, the set of all *infinite words* by A^ω.

Scratch Program. A SCRATCH program App is defined by a set $\mathcal{A}$ of *actors*. There is at most one actor that fills the role of the *stage* and several other actors that are in the *sprites* role [16]. An actor [19] can be instantiated several times; each actor instance is represented by a list of processes. A *concrete state* $c \in C$ of a program is a list of concrete process states $c = \langle p_1, \ldots, p_n \rangle$. A process state $p_i : X \to V$ is a mapping of typed program variables $x \in X$ to their values $v \in V$.

A *concrete program trace* is a sequence $\overline{c} \in C^\infty$ of concrete program states. The set of all possible *concrete program traces* $C^\infty = C^* \cup C^\omega$ consists of the set of finite traces C^* and the set of infinite traces C^ω [19]. The semantics $[\![App]\!]$ of a SCRATCH [16,19] program App are defined by the set of concrete program traces it exhibits, that is, $[\![App]\!] \subseteq C^\infty$.

SCRATCH programs and their actors have a well-defined set of programs with defined meaning, along with user-defined variables. The variables are either actor-local or globally scoped. The set of actor-local variables of sprite actors includes, for example, the variables $\{x, y, direction\}$, which define the position and orientation of a sprite.

Abstract Domain. To cope with the restrictions of reasoning about programs, abstraction is needed [8]. Multiple concrete states can be represented by an abstract state. The *abstract domain* $D = (C, \ddot{E}, \langle\!\langle \cdot \rangle\!\rangle, [\![\cdot]\!], \langle\!\langle \cdot \rangle\!\rangle^{\pi}, \Pi)$ [19] determines the mapping between abstract states E and concrete states C. An *inclusion relation* between the abstract states E is defined by the partial order $\sqsubseteq \subseteq E \times E$ of the *lattice* $\ddot{E} = (E, \sqsubseteq, \sqcup, \sqcap, \top, \bot)$. The mapping between the abstract and concrete world is realized in the *concretization* function $[\![\cdot]\!] : E \to 2^C$ and the *abstraction* function $\langle\!\langle \cdot \rangle\!\rangle : 2^C \to E$. The *widening* function $\langle\!\langle \cdot \rangle\!\rangle^{\pi} : E \times \Pi \to E$ computes an abstraction of a given abstract state by removing irrelevant details according to the *abstraction precision* $\pi \in \Pi$ by defining an equivalence relation $\pi : C \to 2^C$. We also use formulas $\mathcal{F}$ in predicate logic to describe sets of concrete states: a *formula* $\phi \in \mathcal{F}$ denotes $[\![\phi]\!] \subseteq C$ a set of concrete states.

Abstract Reachability Graph. A reachability analysis constructs an abstract reachability graph to determine whether or not a target state is reachable; it proves the absence of such a state if a fixed point is reached, that is, all states have been visited. An *abstract reachability graph* is a directed graph $\mathcal{R} = (E, e_0, \rightsquigarrow)$ of abstract states E rooted in the *initial abstract state* $e_0 \in E$. The structure of the reachability graph $\mathcal{R}$ is determined by its transition relation $\rightsquigarrow \subseteq E \times E$ and we write $e \rightsquigarrow e'$ iff $(e, e') \in \rightsquigarrow$. An *abstract (program) trace* is a finite sequence $\bar{e} = \langle e_0, \ldots, e_{n-1} \rangle$ where each pair $(e, e') \in \bar{e}$ is an element of the transition relation $\rightsquigarrow$. Each abstract (program) trace $\bar{e}$ denotes a possibly infinite set of concrete program traces $[\![\bar{e}]\!] \subseteq C^{\infty}$. An abstract trace is *feasible*, if and only if $[\![\bar{e}]\!] \cap [\![App]\!] \neq \emptyset$, otherwise it is *infeasible*.

Each transition $e \overset{\overline{op}}{\rightsquigarrow} e'$ of the abstract reachability graph can be labeled with a sequence $\overline{op} = \langle op_1, \ldots, op_n \rangle \in Op^*$ of program operations executed to arrive at the abstract successor state e'. The set of program operations Op consists of operations of various types, which can manipulate or check the set of program variables [19]. A SCRATCH block corresponds to a sequence of operations from Op. To simplify the description, we extend Op with call and return operations, where a call represents the beginning of the execution of such a sequence of operations, and a return marks its end.

Static Reachability Analysis. A static analysis (typically) conducts a reachability analysis by creating an overapproximation [8] of all possible states and state sequences of the program under analysis. The resulting abstract reachability graph $\mathcal{R}$ possibly denotes (in case the analysis terminated with a fixed point) a larger set of program traces than the original program has, that is, $[\![App]\!] \subseteq [\![\mathcal{R}]\!]$. An example for a static analysis framework is BASTET [19], which focuses on analyzing SCRATCH programs. An operator $target : E \to 2^S$ determines the set of properties that are considered violated by a given abstract state.

Dynamic Reachability Analysis. Dynamic program analyses are also a form of reachability analysis: The program under execution is steered by an input generator and its behavior is observed by a monitor process. The tool WHISKER [20] guides a SCRATCH program *App* in its original execution environment by sending user inputs or providing mocks for functions that interact with the environment, while observing the resulting behavior of *App*. No abstract semantics are used. In contrast to static reachability analysis the results are always sound.

3 Scratch Error Witnesses

In general, an error witness is an *abstract entity* that describes inputs from the user and the environment to reproduce (to witness) the presence of a specification violation [3]. By not defining all inputs explicitly and keeping them nondeterministic, the degree of abstractness can be varied: An error witness can be *refined* by making more inputs deterministic, and it can be abstracted by increasing nondeterminism. In this work, we aim at error witnesses for SCRATCH programs that can be produced and consumed by both static and dynamic analyses, and that are easy to visualize and follow by users, for example, by novice programmers. SCRATCH error witnesses perform actions that could potentially also be conducted by a user controlling the SCRATCH program manually and provide means to mock parts of the SCRATCH environment to control input sources that would behave nondeterministically otherwise.

Note that while a SCRATCH program can exhibit infinite program traces, the counterexamples and error witnesses we discuss in this work are finite, that is, describing the violation of safety properties—witnessing that something bad (undesired) can happen after finitely many execution steps. We do not consider this to be a practically relevant limitation of our approach since bounded liveness properties—requiring that something good happens within a finite time span—are also safety properties.

A SCRATCH *error witness* is a tuple that defines inputs from the user and the environment to reproduce a specification violation in a particular program. Formally, it is a tuple $(\widetilde{m}, \overline{u}, s) \in W$ consisting of a *mock mapping* $\widetilde{m} : Op \to M$, a finite sequence of timed user interface *inputs* $\overline{u} = \langle u_1, \ldots, u_n \rangle \in U^*$, and the *property* $s \in S$ that is supposed to be violated. The mock mapping is a partial function from the set of operations Op to the mocks M by which to substitute the functionality. A *timed user input* $u = (d, a) \in \mathbb{R} \times A$ is a tuple consisting of an *input delay* $d \geq 0$ in milliseconds, and an *action* $a \in A$ to perform after the delay d elapsed. Note that we abstract from the fact that one mock instance can replace operations of Op of several actor instances. The set of all error witnesses is denoted by W.

For debugging purposes, a timed user input can be enriched by an *expected state condition* $p \in \mathcal{F}$, which is a formula in predicate logic on the state of a SCRATCH program that characterizes the states that are expected to be reached after conducting the action, that is, $[\![p]\!] \subseteq C$. The expected state condition can be used to (1) check if the witness replay steers the program execution to the expected state space region, and to (2) provide details to the user on the sequence of concrete program states leading to the specification violation.

3.1   User Inputs

SCRATCH programs are controlled by the user mainly using mouse and keyboard input actions. To specify possible input actions, we adopt an existing grammar [20] to formulate such actions—with the natural numbers $\mathbb{N}$ and the set of Unicode characters $\mathbb{L}$. An input action $a \in A$ is built based on the following grammar:

$$input = \text{Epsilon} \mid \text{KeyDown } key \mid \text{KeyUp } key \mid \text{MouseDown } pos \mid$$
$$\text{MouseUp } pos \mid \text{MouseMoveTo } pos \mid \text{TextInput } text$$
$$key = \text{keycode } code$$
$$pos = \text{xpos } x \text{ ypos } y$$
$$text = \text{txt } string$$
$$code \in \mathbb{N}, \; string \in \mathbb{L}^*, \; x \in [-240..240], \; y \in [-180..180]$$

3.2   Mocks

Mocks replace specified operations in specified actor instances to control the program execution and steer it towards a target state. Compared to a stub, a *mock* is stateful, that is, the value returned by the mock and side effects can be different from call to call, depending on its *internal state*.

A SCRATCH block (represented by a sequence of operations from Op) that is supposed to return a new random number with each call (a random number generator) is a typical example that has to be mocked to reproduce a particular behavior. That is, any block that leads to some form of nondeterministic program execution is a good candidate to be mocked. SCRATCH allows to add various (custom) extensions—to use SCRATCH for programming hardware components, such as Lego Mindstorms—that add additional variables (or inputs) that require mocking. For example, to sense the motor position, distance, brightness, or acceleration. Even mocking date or time functions might be necessary to reproduce a specific behavior within a dynamic analysis.

We distinguish between different types of mocks. The set of all possible mocks is denoted by the symbol M.

Conditional Effects. A *mock with conditional effects* $(\overline{op}_0, \overline{p}, \overline{\overline{op}}, \overline{r})$ is initialized by a sequence of program operations $\overline{op}_0 \in Op^*$ before its first invocation, describes a sequence of state-space conditions $\overline{p} = \langle p_1, \ldots, p_n \rangle \in \mathcal{F}^*$, and has a sequence of assignment sequences $\overline{\overline{op}} = \langle \overline{op}_1, \ldots, \overline{op}_n \rangle \in (Op^*)^*$ and a sequence of mock return values $\overline{r} = \langle r_1, \ldots, r_n \rangle \in V^*$. An initialization operation $op \in \overline{op}_0$ can, for example, declare and initialize mock-local variables to keep track of the mock's state between different invocations. We require that $|\overline{\overline{op}}| \in \{|\overline{p}|, 0\}$ and $|\overline{r}| \in \{|\overline{p}|, 0\}$ (a mock might not produce a return value, or might not conduct any operations but return a value). In case the current program state c is in one of the regions described by a state-space condition p_i when the mock is invoked, that is, if $c \in [\![p_i]\!]$, then also the operation sequence $\overline{op}_i$ is performed and the value r_i returned. A condition p is a formula in predicate logic over

---

Algorithm 1. testGen(App)

Input: A SCRATCH program App to verify
Output: A set of error witnesses W (empty if the program is safe)
1: (frontier, reached) $\leftarrow$ init$_{App}()$
2: $(\cdot, \text{reached}) \leftarrow$ wrapped(frontier, reached)
3: targets $\leftarrow \{e \mid \text{target}(e) \neq \emptyset \wedge e \in \text{reached}\}$
4: **return** $\bigcup_{t \in \text{targets}}$ toWitness(testify$_1^{\natural}$(reached, t))

---

the program's variables—including those local to the current actor or mock, and global variables. A nondeterministic (random) value is returned in case none of the conditions $p_i \in \bar{p}$ was applicable for an invocation.

Mocks with sequential effects and those with timed effects are specializations of mocks with conditional effects:

Sequential Effects. A *mock with sequential effects* $(\overline{\overline{op}}, \bar{r}) \in (Op^*)^* \times V^*$ describes a sequence of assignment sequences $\overline{\overline{op}} = \langle \overline{op}_1, \ldots, \overline{op}_n \rangle$ and a sequence of mock return values $\bar{r} = \langle r_1, \ldots, r_n \rangle$, both with the same length, that is, $|\overline{\overline{op}}| = |\bar{r}|$. The mock has an internal state variable x that tracks the number of the mock's invocations and corresponds to the position in the sequences. That is, at invocation x, the sequence of assignments $\overline{op}_x$ is performed and the value r_x is returned. A nondeterministic (random) value is returned in case the position x is out of the sequences bounds.

Timed Effects. A *mock with timed effects* $(\bar{y}, \overline{\overline{op}}, \bar{r}) \in (\mathbb{R} \times \mathbb{R})^* \times (Op^*)^* \times V^*$ describes a sequence of disjoint time (in milliseconds) intervals $\bar{y} = \langle y_1, \ldots, y_n \rangle$, a sequence of assignment sequences $\overline{\overline{op}} = \langle \overline{op}_1, \ldots, \overline{op}_n \rangle$, and a sequence of mock return values $\bar{r} = \langle r_1, \ldots, r_n \rangle$. In case the milliseconds $up \in \mathbb{R}$ since the program under test was started is in one of the time intervals y_i, then also the operation sequence $\overline{op}_i$ is performed and the value r_i returned when the mock is invoked.

4 Witness Generation

After we have introduced the notion of a user interface error witness for SCRATCH programs, we now describe how such a witness can be derived from a concrete program trace that violates the specification—which can be recorded by a dynamic analysis tool such as WHISKER and from the abstract reachability graph produced by a static analysis framework such as BASTET.

4.1 Concrete Program Trace from an Abstract Reachability Graph

We first describe how a finite concrete program trace $\bar{c} = \langle c_1, \ldots, c_n \rangle \in C^\infty$ that leads to a (violating) target state $e_t \in E$, with target$(e_t) \neq \emptyset \wedge c_n \in [\![e_t]\!]$, can be extracted from an abstract reachability graph. This process is typically implemented in a procedure for model checking or model-based test generation.

The outermost algorithm of a model checker with test generation is outlined in Algorithm 1. All abstract states that have been reached by the analysis can be found in the set reached $\subseteq E$, the set frontier $\subseteq$ reached contains all abstract states from which successor states remain to be explored. These sets are initialized by the operator init with the *initial abstract states* to analyze the program *App*. The actual reachability analysis is performed by the wrapped algorithm, represented by the method wrapped, which can, for example, conduct an analysis based on predicate abstraction [13] and counterexample-guided abstraction refinement [7]. This wrapped (pseudo) algorithm terminates when it has reached a fixed point without reaching a violating state or after one or more violations have been identified. The set targets $\subseteq F$ contains all states that violate the specification.

An abstract reachability graph $\mathcal{R} = (E, e_0, \rightsquigarrow)$ describes the predecessor-successor-relation of the states in this set—represented by the transfer relation $\rightsquigarrow \subseteq E \times E$. An abstract state represents a set of concrete states, that is, $[\![e]\!] \subseteq C$. A sequence $\bar{e} = \langle e_0, \ldots, e_{n-1} \rangle \in E^*$ of abstract states that starts in an initial abstract state e_0 and that is well-founded in the transfer relation $\rightsquigarrow$ is called an *abstract program trace*. An abstract program trace $\bar{e}$ represents a set of concrete program traces, i.e., $[\![\bar{e}]\!] \subseteq C^*$. That is, to get to a concrete program trace $\bar{c}$ that reaches a target state $e \in E$, we first have to select a feasible abstract program trace from graph $\mathcal{R}$, and can then concretize this trace. An abstract program trace is called *feasible* if it denotes at least one concrete program trace. Note that an abstract reachability graph can also contain abstract states that do not have a counterpart in the real world, that is, which are infeasible.

Generic Analysis Operators. We define a list of new analysis operators in line with the configurable program analysis framework [5,19] to extract abstract program traces and concrete program traces from a given set of reached states, reaching a target state:

1. The *abstract testification operator* testify : $2^E \times E \to 2^{E^*}$ returns a collection of abstract program traces. Given a set of abstract states $R \subseteq$ reached and a target state $e_t \in E$, this analysis operator returns only *feasible* program traces—describing only *feasible sequences* of abstract states, all starting in an initial abstract state, and all leading to the given target state e_t. That is, all infeasible traces that would lead to the target are eliminated by this operator. An empty collection is returned in case the given target state is infeasible.

   The *abstract single testification operator* testify$_1$: $2^E \times E \to 2^{E^*}$ strengthens the operator testify and describes *at most one feasible* abstract program trace.

2. The *concrete testification operator* testify$^\natural$: $2^E \times E \to 2^{C^*}$ returns all *concrete* program traces reaching a given target state. Note that, assuming unbounded value domains, this collection can have infinitely many elements.

   The *concrete single testification operator* is supposed to return at most one concrete program trace that reaches the given target state and has the signature testify$_1^\natural$: $2^E \times E \to 2^{C \times C}$.

Algorithm 2. toWitness : $C^* \rightarrow 2^W$

Input: A concrete program trace $\bar{c} \in C^*$
Output: A set of error witnesses $\in 2^W$
1: $\tilde{m} \leftarrow$ constructMocks($\bar{c}$)
2: $\bar{u} \leftarrow$ constructInputSeq($\bar{c}$)
3: **return** $\{(\tilde{m}, \bar{u}, s) \mid s \in$ target(t)$\}$

Algorithm 3. constructInputSeq$_{Ax}$: $C^* \rightarrow U^*$

Input: A concrete program trace $\bar{c} \in C^*$
Output: A timed input sequence $\in U^*$
1: $\bar{\bar{a}} \leftarrow \langle\rangle$
2: **for** (op, c) **in** $\Gamma(\bar{c})$ **do**
3:    $\bar{\bar{u}} \leftarrow \bar{\bar{a}} \circ \langle$choose($\{ \text{ax}(op, c) \mid \text{ax} \in \text{Ax} \}$)$\rangle$
4: **return** foldEpsilonDelays($\bar{\bar{a}}, \bar{c}$)

Note that these operators do not guarantee any particular strategy for choosing abstract or concrete program traces. Nevertheless, different implementations or parameterizations of these operators can be provided that realize different strategies—contributing to the idea of configurable program analysis.

Operator Implementations. The implementations of the testification operators vary depending on the composed analysis procedure and its abstract domain—see the literature [5,19] for details on composing analyses. We provide a first implementation of these operators in the BASTET program analysis framework, in which program traces are chosen arbitrarily.

For a bounded model-checking configuration that does not compute any (block) abstractions, concrete program traces can be produced simply by asking an SMT solver for a satisfying assignment (a model) for a formula with which a violating state is supposed to be reached.

4.2   Error Witness from a Concrete Program Trace

We now describe how SCRATCH error witnesses $(\tilde{m}, \bar{u}, s) \in W$ can be produced from a given finite concrete program trace $\bar{c} = \langle c_1, \ldots, c_n \rangle \in C^*$. Such a trace can be created from a model checking run using one of the proposed testification operators, or can be created from the states observed while running the program on a machine, e.g., along with a dynamic analysis. Algorithm 2 outlines the process of generating a SCRATCH error witness from a concrete program trace.

We assume that there is a transition labelling function $\Gamma : C \times C \rightarrow Op^*$ for labelling state transitions. Given a pair $c_1, c_2 \in C$ of concrete states, the function returns a (possibly empty) sequence $\langle op_1, \ldots, op_n \rangle$ of program operations conducted to reach from state c_1 to state c_2. We extend the labelling function to sequences, resulting in an overloaded version $\Gamma : C^* \rightarrow (Op \times C)^*$ that produces sequences of pairs of program operations and concrete (successor) states; the first concrete state in the given concrete program trace is skipped.

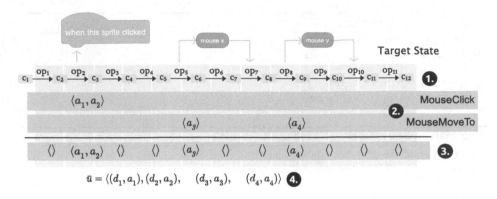

Fig. 2. Generation of the sequence of timed inputs in BASTET

Algorithm 4. constructMocks$_{\mathrm{Mx}}$: $C^* \to 2^{Op \times M}$

Input: A concrete program trace $\bar{c} \in C^*$
Output: A mock mapping $\subseteq Op \times M$
1: **return** $\{\mathrm{mx}(\bar{c}, \Gamma(\bar{c})) \mid \mathrm{mx} \in \mathrm{Mx}\}$

Timed Inputs. A witness contains the sequence of timed user inputs $\bar{u} = \langle u_1, \ldots, u_n \rangle \in U^*$, where each element $u_i = (d, a) \in \bar{u}$ consists of a delay $d \in \mathbb{R}$ (in milliseconds) to wait before conducting an input action a. Algorithm 3 outlines the process of creating this sequence and Fig. 2 provides a visual perspective on the process and the example to discuss. The algorithm is implicitly parameterized with a collection of action extractors Ax. Generally, there is one action extractor $ax \in Ax$ for each class of input action—see the grammar of input actions in Sect. 3.1. In our example, we use ② an extractor for the action MouseMoveTo and a *composite* action extractor MouseClick that produces two different actions (MouseDown and MouseUp, resulting in a "mouse click").

The algorithm starts from a given ① concrete program trace $\bar{c} \in C^*$ leading to a target state that violates one or more properties $\subseteq S$. The trace is traversed from its start to the end (with the target) state, and the action extractors are invoked along this trace. A call to the action extractor for a given concrete state c that is reached by a program operation op returns a sequence of input actions $\bar{a}$ to execute at this point in the resulting witness. For example, the actions $\langle a_1, a_2 \rangle$ are produced by the MouseClick action extractor for the operation op_2 reaching state c_3, with $a_1 = $ MouseDown xpos 23 ypos 8 and $a_2 = $ MouseUp xpos 23 ypos 8. This action sequence is emitted because operation op_2 signaled a click to the sprite, the mouse position is extracted from the concrete state c_3. MouseMove actions are produced whenever the mouse is expected to be on a particular position, for example, queried by a $\boxed{\text{mouse x}}$ or $\boxed{\text{mouse y}}$ SCRATCH block. The result ③ of applying the action extractors along the trace is a sequence $\bar{\bar{a}} \in A^{**}$ of sequences of input actions. In case multiple action extractors provide a non-empty sequence for a particular position

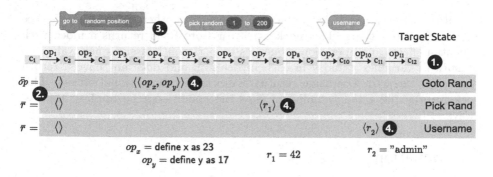

Fig. 3. Generation of mocks in BASTET

along the trace, the operator choose chooses an action sequence based on priorities. In the last step **4.**, empty elements (containing an empty sequence) are eliminated from $\overline{\overline{a}}$ and a delay is added that determines how long to wait before executing a particular action. This functionality is provided by the function foldEpsilonDelays.

Mock Mappings. A SCRATCH error witness contains a mock mapping $\widetilde{m}$: $Op \to M$, which specifies mocks used for substituting particular operations of the program or the runtime environment to steer a program execution (or a state space traversal) towards a target state that violates the specification.

The creation of the mocks from a given concrete program trace is implemented in the function constructMocks, which is outlined in Algorithm 4. The algorithm is implicitly parameterized by a list of mock extractors Mx. A *mock extractor* is a function that creates a mock for a SCRATCH block or a function of the runtime environment based on a given trace. Section 3.2 already motivated why we need mocks for SCRATCH programs, and discussed mocks with different degrees of expressiveness. Typically, we have one mock extractor for each block that interacts with the environment (the operating system, the runtime environment, connected hardware components).

Figure 3 illustrates the process of generating mocks based on a given concrete program trace **1.** leading to a target state, which violates one or more properties $\subseteq S$. Three mock extractors are in place: Goto Rand produces a mock for the SCRATCH block go to random position, Pick Rand produces a mock for pick random (..) to (..), and Username produces a mock for the block username. All mock extractors operate by consuming the input trace from left-to-right, starting with an empty mock **2.**, and then enriching it from step-to-step. In contrast to action extractors, mock extractors determine their behavior *after* the observed block returns **3.** to the calling block, then, the mock is updated based on the concrete state found at that point in the trace **4.**.

Note that each mock extractor can produce another type of mock—see Sect. 3.2 for mock types. The mock extractor Goto Rand returns a mock with sequential effects and operation sequences to perform: It assigns new values to the sprite's variables x and y in each invocation, and does not have a return value. The extractor Username returns a mock with conditional effects: This mock returns the value "admin" in case the condition *true* applies, that is, always.

5 Evaluation

We illustrate the practicality of generating and replaying (validating) UI error witnesses for SCRATCH programs. In particular, we are interested if our concepts are *effective* and if they contribute to a more *efficient* tool chain to show the presence of bugs in UI centered programs.

5.1 Experiment Setup

Implementation. We implemented the concepts presented in this paper in the static program analysis framework BASTET [19] and in the dynamic analysis tool WHISKER [20]. We added support to generate error witnesses from an abstract reachability graph into BASTET, and enriched WHISKER with support for replaying these witnesses. We also defined a witness exchange format based on JSON to exchange error witnesses between analysis tools.

Benchmarking Environment. Students and teachers in educational contexts such as schools typically do not have access to large computing clusters. For this reason, we tried to aim for a more practical setting and conducted our experiments on a single desktop workstation featuring an Intel(R) Core(TM) i7-2600 processor with 3.40 GHz and 32 GiB of RAM (although as little as 2 to 4 GiB would have been sufficient for our case study). The machine runs Debian GNU/Linux 10 and the current LTS version of Node.js (v14.16.0 at the time of writing). Our additions to support SCRATCH error witness generation are implemented in BASTET (version af0a20db) and its replay in WHISKER (version 392712bf). We used the Node.js API provided by Puppeteer[1] to control a browser and automatically stimulate our case study SCRATCH programs with user input.

Case Study. SCRATCH is backed by a large online ecosystem and community. For example, Code Club[2] is a global network of free coding clubs for 9 to 13 year-olds with the aim of helping children develop programming skills in SCRATCH, among other languages. We took inspiration from one of their SCRATCH projects called "Brain Game"[3] and use it as a case study.

---

[1] https://github.com/puppeteer/puppeteer.

[2] https://codeclub.org/en.

[3] https://projects.raspberrypi.org/en/projects/brain-game-cc.

Fig. 4. The Brain Game example program (Color figure online)

Here, the task is to implement a game with a quiz master asking the player for the result of five randomly chosen arithmetic computations (see Fig. 4). Only a correct answer increases the player's score. The game ends when all questions were answered correctly (in which case a green check mark sprite is displayed) or when a wrong answer was given (in which case a black cross appears).

We chose Brain Game because its size and complexity are typical of the programs developed by learners. Moreover, it exhibits randomness and requires user interaction, which is challenging for program analysis tools.

Afterwards, we devised four properties that constitute our notion of a correct Brain Game implementation:

P1. The score must have been initialized with 0 before the first question is asked.
P2. The green check mark must be shown within 200 ms when all questions were answered correctly.
P3. The black cross must be shown within 200 ms when a question was answered incorrectly.
P4. The score must not decrease.

We formalized these properties as both LEILA [19] programs and WHISKER tests. The former can be fed to BASTET with the aim of checking a given program against this specification and generating an error witness, and the latter is handed to WHISKER to verify the error witness. We implemented five erroneous variants V1–V5, each violating one of the above properties:

V1. Violates P1: the score is not initialized at all.
V2. Violates P2: the sprite for the wrong answer is not shown when a question was answered incorrectly.
V3. Violates P3: the sprite for the correct answer is not shown when all five questions were answered correctly.
V4. Violates P4: the score decreases by one when an incorrect answer is given.
V5. Violates P4: the score decreases by one when an incorrect answer is given *except* when it would turn negative.

Table 1. Effectiveness, execution times in seconds rounded to two significant digits

Variant	Replay successful?	Replay time
V1	×	2.953
V2	✓	4.036
V3	✓	7.997
V4	✓	4.099
V5	✓	5.010

5.2   Witness Replay and Validation (Effectiveness)

Effectiveness describes the ability to replay and validate the statically generated witnesses by a dynamic analysis. To this end, we ran each of the five erroneous Brain Game variants along with the specification in BASTET and extracted the error witnesses. Then, we ran WHISKER together with the specification and the SCRATCH error witness on each program under test to investigate if the witness generated by BASTET can be verified in WHISKER.

The results are summarized in Table 1 and show that four out of five errors were reproducible. In detail, the violations of properties P2–P4 by programs V2–V5 were revealed via static analysis by BASTET and confirmed by dynamic replay in WHISKER. V2 and V4 both require a wrong answer for the fault to be exposed. P3 requires five correct answers. Finally, V5 requires at least one correct answer followed by a wrong answer.

While V2–V5 were validated successfully, the tools disagree when it comes to the violation of property P1 by variant V1: BASTET detected a violation but this could not be confirmed by WHISKER. When first reading the score variable, BASTET detects that it has not been initialized yet, thus deeming its usage unsafe and reporting a violation. This requires no user interaction and the generated replay contains no user input. When replaying the generated witness in WHISKER, however, no violation is detected. This is because uninitialized variables in SCRATCH have a default value of 0 before the first program execution, which just so happens to be the value demanded by the specification. However, the violation *could* be detected by WHISKER when at least one correct answer is given (thus increasing the score to at least 1) and the game is played for a second time, where the score would still be 1 as it is not reset from the previous game.

The failure to detect V1 highlights a limitation in our work: the current definition of a SCRATCH error witness only allows for mock mappings but not for setting the initial state of a SCRATCH program. While the formalism in Sect. 3 can be easily extended, more implementation work in WHISKER is necessary to support this. We plan to address both issues in future work.

We conclude that SCRATCH error witness reuse among different tools is possible, but may reveal differences in implicit assumptions or approximations.

Table 2. Efficiency for different verification tasks, execution times in seconds rounded to two significant digits

Variant	Error witness generation and replay				Random input generation (estimated)
	Analysis	Concretization	Replay	Combined	
V1	25	0.52	3.0	28	400
V2	50	0.83	4.0	54	400
V3	1500	10	8.0	1500	7.6×10^{10}
V4	47	1.0	4.1	51	400
V5	210	2.1	5.0	220	500

5.3   Sequential Tool Combination (Efficiency)

The second question we investigate is whether guiding a dynamic analysis by tests generated from a static analysis can increase the testing efficiency. For this purpose, we measured the combined execution times of BASTET and WHISKER to generate and replay an error witness, and compare it against the expected average runtime of WHISKER when purely unguided random input generation were to be used. Table 2 contains the results of this experiment.

Looking at the combined times in Table 2, we see that the fault in program variant V1 is easiest to reveal for BASTET since it requires no user interaction. V2 and V4 entail similar effort, both require one wrong answer. V5 requires a wrong and a correct answer and poses more challenges to BASTET, increasing verification time by one order of magnitude. V3 requires 5 correct answers; as this requires covering more program states, the additional analysis effort increases the time by another order of magnitude.

To contrast this with the time it would take to reveal the faults using only random input generation in WHISKER, we consider the average expected execution time of this inherently randomized approach: The space of possible answers to each question asked in Brain Game consists of $200 - 2 = 198$ numbers. (The two summands range between 1 and 100). In the best case scenario, WHISKER manages to generate the correct answer on the first try. In the worst case scenario, there is no upper limit to how many tries are necessary. However, assuming that the random number generator produces evenly distributed numbers the average number of tries can be computed as $198/2 = 99$. Moreover, from Table 2 we can infer that a SCRATCH error witness replay for one question takes roughly 4 s. With this, the average execution time can be estimated as $4 \times 99 = 396$ s for V2 and V4. Similarly, for V5 (which requires one correct and one wrong answer), a wrong answer is given in one try on average but replay lasts longer (5 s). Thus, the estimated time is $5 \times (99 \times 1) = 495$ s.

Table 3. Scaling experiment conducted on differently sized variants of program V3, execution times in seconds rounded to two significant digits

Variant	Analysis	Concretization	Replay	Combined
$V3_1$	57	0.90	5.9	63
$V3_2$	170	2.4	5.2	170
$V3_3$	410	4.7	6.0	420
$V3_4$	810	7.0	7.0	820
$V3_5$	1500	10	8.0	1500

To reveal the fault in V1, however, we would require at least one correct answer, followed by a restart of the game. The replay time for this cannot be extracted from the table (since we did not have user interaction) but using a conservative estimation of 4 s, similar to V2 and V4, the estimated execution time is also 396 s. Exposing the fault in V3 requires 5 correct answers in a row. An average number of 99^5 tries with a replay time of 8 s results in a total runtime of 7.6×10^{10} s, which is more than 2400 years.

While these results suggest the combined approach is more efficient, this depends on how BASTET's performance scales with increasing size of the programs to generate error witnesses for. We therefore analyze the impact of the size of the state space in BASTET on the verification time using four alternate versions $V3_1$, $V3_2$, $V3_3$ and $V3_4$ of V3 requiring one, two, three and four correct answers instead of five, respectively. We use $V3_5$ synonymously for V3. Afterwards, we generated error witnesses for each of the four new variants using BASTET. The run times are presented in Table 3. For each additional question asked, the results indicate that the verification time increases linearly by a factor of 2. Since error witness generation dominates the costs, the same increase can also be seen for the combined execution time.

Overall, the results indicate that guiding a dynamic analysis by tests generated from a static analysis can increase the testing efficiency, and scales well with increasing test program size.

6   Related Work

As it can be beneficial to hide the internal models of analysis and verification tools to support adoption by users or developers [21], the idea of producing executable tests from counterexamples has been revisited in different contexts over time. An early approach to produce executable tests from counterexamples [2] was implemented for the BLAST model checker [14], and many alternative approaches followed. For example, Rocha et al. [18] generate executable programs for counterexamples produced for C programs by ESBMC [9], Muller and Ruskiewicz [17] produce .NET executables from Spec# programs and symbolic counterexamples, Csallner and Smaragdakis [10] produce Java tests for counterexamples generated by ESC/Java [11], and Beyer et al. [4] presented an approach that converts verification results produced by CPAChecker [6] to executable C code. Our approach applies similar principles, but considers interactive, graphical programs, where verification tasks consider possible sequences of user interactions. Executable error witnesses for interactive programs with user interactions need to mock not only user inputs, but also other environmental dependencies. Gennari et al. [12] described an approach that also builds mock environments, but again targets C programs. Besides the interactive nature of UI error witnesses, a further property that distinguishes our problem from prior work is that we are considering timed traces. Timed counterexamples are produced, for example, by Kronos [22, 23] or Uppaal-Tron [15]; however, we are not aware of any approaches to produce executable tests from such counterexamples. Testification of error witnesses has not only been proposed for producing executable tests, but also as an interchange format for different verification tools [3]; again a main difference of our approach is that our interchange format considers UI error witnesses rather than C function invocations. Aljazzar and Leue [1] produced interactive visualizations of counterexamples to support debugging. By producing UI tests from UI error witnesses we achieve a similar goal: Users can observe program executions and the interactions with the program along described by the error witness.

7 Conclusions

This paper introduced the notion of error witnesses for programs with graphical user interfaces—controlled by mouse and keyboard inputs, sent at particular points in time. We illustrated our concepts and implementation in the context of the analysis of game-like programs that were developed using visual- and block-based programming, in SCRATCH. We (1) formalized the notion of UI error witnesses, (2) described how these witnesses can be generated from the abstract reachability graph that was constructed with an SMT-based (Satisfiability Modulo Theories) software model checker, and (3) demonstrated their practicality for confirming the presence of errors in a dynamic analysis.

The exchange of error witnesses between different verification tools opens up possibilities to develop hybrid approaches that increase efficiency. Our findings also indicate that error witnesses can be useful in order to cross-check and test tools. Besides the technical aspects, however, there also remains the larger problem of making UI error witnesses accessible and useful for learning programmers.

References

1. Aljazzar, H., Leue, S.: Debugging of dependability models using interactive visualization of counterexamples. In: QEST, pp. 189–198. IEEE Computer Society (2008)
2. Beyer, D., Chlipala, A., Henzinger, T.A., Jhala, R., Majumdar, R.: Generating tests from counterexamples. In: ICSE, pp. 326–335. IEEE Computer Society (2004)

3. Beyer, D., Dangl, M., Dietsch, D., Heizmann, M., Stahlbauer, A.: Witness validation and stepwise testification across software verifiers. In: ESEC/SIGSOFT FSE, pp. 721–733. ACM (2015)
4. Beyer, D., Dangl, M., Lemberger, T., Tautschnig, M.: Tests from witnesses. In: Dubois, C., Wolff, B. (eds.) TAP 2018. LNCS, vol. 10889, pp. 3–23. Springer, Cham (2018). https://doi.org/10.1007/978-3-319-92994-1_1
5. Beyer, D., Henzinger, T.A., Théoduloz, G.: Configurable software verification: concretizing the convergence of model checking and program analysis. In: Damm, W., Hermanns, H. (eds.) CAV 2007. LNCS, vol. 4590, pp. 504–518. Springer, Heidelberg (2007). https://doi.org/10.1007/978-3-540-73368-3_51
6. Beyer, D., Keremoglu, M.E.: CPAchecker: a tool for configurable software verification. CoRR abs/0902.0019 (2009)
7. Clarke, E., Grumberg, O., Jha, S., Lu, Y., Veith, H.: Counterexample-guided abstraction refinement. In: Emerson, E.A., Sistla, A.P. (eds.) CAV 2000. LNCS, vol. 1855, pp. 154–169. Springer, Heidelberg (2000). https://doi.org/10.1007/10722167_15
8. Clarke, E.M., Grumberg, O., Long, D.E.: Model checking and abstraction. ACM Trans. Program. Lang. Syst. 16(5), 1512–1542 (1994)
9. Cordeiro, L., Fischer, B., Marques-Silva, J.: SMT-based bounded model checking for embedded ANSI-C software. IEEE Trans. Softw. Eng. 38(4), 957–974 (2011)
10. Csallner, C., Smaragdakis, Y.: Check 'n' Crash: combining static checking and testing. In: Proceedings of the 27th International Conference on Software Engineering, pp. 422–431 (2005)
11. Flanagan, C., Leino, K.R.M., Lillibridge, M., Nelson, G., Saxe, J.B., Stata, R.: Extended static checking for Java. In: Proceedings of the ACM SIGPLAN 2002 Conference on Programming Language Design and Implementation, pp. 234–245 (2002)
12. Gennari, J., Gurfinkel, A., Kahsai, T., Navas, J.A., Schwartz, E.J.: Executable counterexamples in software model checking. In: Piskac, R., Rümmer, P. (eds.) VSTTE 2018. LNCS, vol. 11294, pp. 17–37. Springer, Cham (2018). https://doi.org/10.1007/978-3-030-03592-1_2
13. Graf, S., Saidi, H.: Construction of abstract state graphs with PVS. In: Grumberg, O. (ed.) CAV 1997. LNCS, vol. 1254, pp. 72–83. Springer, Heidelberg (1997). https://doi.org/10.1007/3-540-63166-6_10
14. Henzinger, T.A., Jhala, R., Majumdar, R., Sutre, G.: Lazy abstraction. In: Proceedings of the 29th ACM SIGPLAN-SIGACT Symposium on Principles of Programming Languages, pp. 58–70 (2002)
15. Larsen, K.G., Mikucionis, M., Nielsen, B., Skou, A.: Testing real-time embedded software using UPPAAL-TRON: an industrial case study. In: EMSOFT, pp. 299–306. ACM (2005)
16. Maloney, J., Resnick, M., Rusk, N., Silverman, B., Eastmond, E.: The scratch programming language and environment. ACM Trans. Comput. Educ. 10(4), 16:1–16:15 (2010)
17. Müller, P., Ruskiewicz, J.N.: Using debuggers to understand failed verification attempts. In: Butler, M., Schulte, W. (eds.) FM 2011. LNCS, vol. 6664, pp. 73–87. Springer, Heidelberg (2011). https://doi.org/10.1007/978-3-642-21437-0_8
18. Rocha, H., Barreto, R., Cordeiro, L., Neto, A.D.: Understanding programming bugs in ANSI-C software using bounded model checking counter-examples. In: Derrick, J., Gnesi, S., Latella, D., Treharne, H. (eds.) IFM 2012. LNCS, vol. 7321, pp. 128–142. Springer, Heidelberg (2012). https://doi.org/10.1007/978-3-642-30729-4_10

19. Stahlbauer, A., Frädrich, C., Fraser, G.: Verified from scratch: program analysis for learners' programs. In: ASE. IEEE (2020)
20. Stahlbauer, A., Kreis, M., Fraser, G.: Testing scratch programs automatically. In: ESEC/SIGSOFT FSE, pp. 165–175. ACM (2019)
21. Visser, W., Dwyer, M.B., Whalen, M.W.: The hidden models of model checking. Softw. Syst. Model. **11**(4), 541–555 (2012). https://doi.org/10.1007/s10270-012-0281-9
22. Yovine, S.: Model checking timed automata. In: Rozenberg, G., Vaandrager, F.W. (eds.) EEF School 1996. LNCS, vol. 1494, pp. 114–152. Springer, Heidelberg (1998). https://doi.org/10.1007/3-540-65193-4_20
23. Yovine, S.: KRONOS: a verification tool for real-time systems. Int. J. Softw. Tools Technol. Transfer **1**(1–2), 123–133 (1997). https://doi.org/10.1007/s100090050009

Using a Guided Fuzzer and Preconditions to Achieve Branch Coverage with Valid Inputs

Amirfarhad Nilizadeh[1]([⊠]), Gary T. Leavens[1],
and Corina S. Păsăreanu[2]

[1] University of Central Florida,
Orlando, FL, USA
af.nilizadeh@knights.ucf.edu
[2] NASA Ames Research Center, Carnegie Mellon University,
Moffett Field, Mountain View, CA, USA

Abstract. Software is widely used in critical systems. Thus, it is important that developers can quickly find semantic bugs with testing; however, semantic bugs can only be revealed by tests that use valid inputs. Guided fuzzers can create input tests that cover all branches; however, they may not necessarily cover all branches with valid inputs. Therefore, the problem is how to guide a fuzzer to cover all branches in a program with only valid inputs. We perform a study of an idea that guarantees that all inputs generated by a guided fuzzer that reach the program under test are valid using formal specifications and runtime assertion checking. Our results show that this idea improves the feedback given to a guided fuzzer.

Keywords: Guided fuzzing · Testing · Branch coverage · Valid inputs · Formal methods · Runtime assertion checking

1 Introduction

Two effective techniques for discovering software vulnerabilities are runtime assertion checking [15,34,42,45] and guided fuzzing [43,44,48].

Runtime assertion checking (RAC) checks formal specifications during testing a program to dynamically detect violations of a program's specified behavior. However, formal specifications are conditional; only if inputs satisfy a program's precondition does it make sense to run the program and check for semantic bugs by checking the program's postcondition. That is, a *semantic bug* is a program behavior that fails to satisfy the program's postcondition when started in an input state that satisfies the program's precondition. Thus for finding semantic bugs, valid inputs for the program's entry method are essential. Moreover,

© Springer Nature Switzerland AG 2021
F. Loulergue and F. Wotawa (Eds.): TAP 2021, LNCS 12740, pp. 72–84, 2021.
https://doi.org/10.1007/978-3-030-79379-1_5

to maximize the chances of finding semantic bugs, test suites should be high-quality; a high-quality test suite would cover all branches in a program.

One way to create high-quality test suites is to use a guided fuzzing tool. *Guided fuzzing* is the process of using feedback from test runs to generate inputs that may cover more branches in hopes of leading to a program crash. However, guided fuzzers (such as AFL [66]) may generate many invalid inputs, which are useless for finding semantic bugs; furthermore, running a program with invalid inputs sometimes is very time-consuming and can lead to infinite loops.

Most guided fuzzer tools work with a driver that translates generated input data from the fuzzer to the program's input types. The driver can use that input data to generate valid inputs for the program. However, such drivers do not guarantee that all inputs are valid. Therefore, the problem we address is how to work with a guided fuzzer so that it only runs the program under test (PUT) with valid inputs. Different methods have been proposed for filtering invalid inputs from a fuzzer, like taint analysis [58] and machine learning [25]. However, these techniques do not guarantee that they will catch and ignore all invalid inputs. Thus invalid inputs may slow the process of running the tests. We guarantee that the PUT will not be executed on invalid input. Our work confirms previous work [18,33,36,53] that emphasizes the importance of providing valid inputs to help guided fuzzers, making the testing process more efficient and effective.

To solve this problem, we propose combining formal precondition speci-fications with a guided fuzzer and demonstrate this idea by combining the JML formal behavioral specification language [9,37–41] with the guided fuzzer Kelinci [33,52,53]. We call this combination JMLKelinci, as it uses JML's RAC (OpenJML) [16,17] to test a program's preconditions and a Java version of AFL [66], namely Kelinci [33], to generate tests. While in this paper we use JML to specify preconditions and Kelinci as the guided fuzzer, our idea could be implemented with other formal specification languages and guided fuzzers.

Given a program P and its precondition, *Pre*, an input is *valid for P* if the input satisfies *Pre*; otherwise, the input is *invalid*. For example, consider a factorial program with a precondition that the input should be an integer number between 0 and 20 (to avoid overflow). An input of 6 would be a valid input, while an input of 21 would be invalid.

Our idea is to guide the fuzzer by dynamically checking each of the generated inputs using a RAC; all invalid inputs are directed to a single branch in the program's driver. Thus when the guided fuzzer tries to cover all branches, it will try to avoid such invalid inputs. JMLKelinci only executes programs on valid inputs; thus, it acts like a guided fuzzer that only generates valid inputs. We note that if a formal specification is available, one can use a verification tool instead of a fuzzer. However, successful use of a static verification tool, such as JML's extended static checker [12,16,17], requires much more effort, such as more detailed specifications, than are needed for JML's RAC. For verification, one needs to write, for example, loop invariants, which are not needed to use RAC successfully. In particular, writing a precondition and postcondition is much simpler than writing all of the specifications needed for static verification. Indeed, JMLKelinci can filter invalid inputs using only a precondition for the entry method of the program being tested (and any needed constructors). Thus even preconditions are not needed for all methods in the program; this reduces the amount of effort needed to use preconditions and a guided fuzzer. Furthermore, some tools can infer preconditions for JML automatically [19,49].

Our results show that JMLKelinci covers all branches of the program under test with valid inputs, which is a first step towards using the benefits of both RAC and a guided fuzzer to detect semantic bugs. However, Kelinci cannot cover all branches for programs with nontrivial[1] preconditions. Also, JMLKelinci covers branches faster than standard Kelinci for some programs with nontrivial preconditions, because running invalid tests can be very time-consuming. In sum, our preliminary results with JMLKelinci indicate that, when combined with postcondition checking, the combination of a guided fuzzer and a RAC can detect many kinds of semantic bugs instead of only finding semantic bugs that lead to a program crash.

2   Related Work

Various authors have presented approaches to generating valid inputs. Gode-froid et al. [25] used machine learning in a grammar-based fuzzer to generate a grammar for the program under test (PUT) to create valid inputs. Rajpal et al. [57] proposed using deep learning to predict which bytes of selected inputs should be mutated to create a valid input. TaintScope [62] uses taint analysis to bypass invalid inputs. However, while these approaches increase the probability of generating valid inputs, they do not guarantee them.

Several network protocol fuzzers provide a specification or grammar of the input structure, like SNOOZE [3] and TFuzz [32]. Some Kernel API fuzzers provide templates that specify the number and types of input arguments, like syzkaller [30]. Furthermore, some fuzzers are designed for a specific language, and the model of language with its specification is built into the fuzzer for generating valid inputs, like funfuzz [35] for JavaScript. By contrast, our idea is not limited to particular input structure formats or languages but can work with any programming language for which one can formally specify preconditions.

Several works [13,14,56,64,67] use a RAC to decide if tests pass, but require users to generate their own test data or only provide a small amount of test data. These works do not attempt to achieve branch coverage.

Some other tools [1,2,4,6,8,10,23,24,46,61] use symbolic execution and/or model checking to generate input tests. However, they do not use branch coverage metrics; because these tools use model checking their execution time depends on the size of the PUT, so they have limited scalability.

Korat [5,47] is similar to our work in that it uses JML preconditions for val-idating inputs. However, while Korat can automatically create inputs that are

---

[1] An assertion is *trivial* if it is always true.

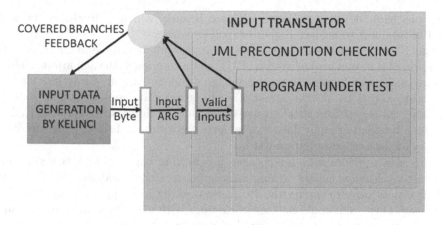

Fig. 1. The architecture of JMLKelinci

complex data structures, Korat does not measure branch coverage or attempt to increase it. Furthermore, Korat has limited scalability. Future work could consider combining Korat's techniques with ours, perhaps enabling a more automatic synthesis of complex inputs for testing.

Some recent studies [11,53,59,60] have combined fuzzing with symbolic execution. These works add tests generated using symbolic execution to the pool of (interesting) inputs that guide the fuzzer. However, they cannot guarantee that all generated inputs are valid.

The following tools measure code coverage and attempt to improve it when generating test suites: EvoSuite [20–22], Randoop [54,55], and TSTL [26,27,29]. However, they cannot guarantee that only valid inputs are passed to the PUT. TSTL allows the specification of invariant properties that must hold during testing, but not preconditions. Randoop can document program behavior with assertions, but does not filter inputs based on user-specified preconditions, which would guarantee that only valid inputs are passed to the PUT.

3   JMLKelinci

To demonstrate our idea for combining formal methods with a fuzzer, we developed a prototype tool, JMLKelinci, that acts like a guided fuzzer but only generates valid inputs by combining Kelinci and JML's RAC tool. As shown in Fig. 1, the prototype tool uses the guided fuzzer, Kelinci, to generate input data and runs the PUT with JML's RAC tool. The user writes a driver for the PUT that takes the input data (bytes generated by Kelinci), converts them to the types of inputs needed by the PUT (program arguments), and then runs the PUT using JML's RAC tool. If the converted inputs do not pass the specified precondition, then the driver catches the precondition violation exception thrown by JML's RAC and returns (normally). This precondition checking guarantees that no invalid inputs are passed to the body of the PUT. Furthermore, all precondition violations lead the program down a single branch, which Kelinci thus tries to avoid in its quest to achieve higher branch coverage.

The Kelinci tool in our prototype generates input data and monitors the execution of the combined driver and PUT when running with each input. Kelinci tries to reach the highest branch coverage (and find input data that lead to uncaught exceptions or other crashes). The generated input data that lead to new branches (or such crashes) are saved in a pool of "interesting" inputs. Kelinci uses such interesting input data in a genetic algorithm to help it generate other such input data using byte mutation.

Our idea provides four advantages for fuzzing compared to the standard Kelinci tool. First, it makes testing more efficient since it catches and bypasses invalid inputs before running the PUT. Second, by avoiding covering branches with invalid inputs, it could find semantic bugs with valid inputs. Third, because the pool of interesting tests consists of valid inputs (except for at most one invalid input) the genetic algorithm used by Kelinci has an increased probability of generating other valid inputs; this should result in achieving branch coverage of the PUT with valid inputs more efficiently [63,65]. Finally, the initial seed for the fuzzer can be chosen with fewer restrictions. The initial seed for Kelinci must be an input that does not lead to an infinite loop or a crash, but when combined with JML, this property is guaranteed even if the initial input is invalid.

As with other guided fuzzers, with JMLKelinci a tester must write a driver to generate valid inputs. Thus, what is the reason for using precondition checking? Using precondition checking guarantees that the PUT will always execute with valid inputs. At the same time, a driver might not consider all program preconditions, so a guided fuzzer using a driver might still generate invalid inputs. Furthermore, as we will show in the next section, when a driver always generates valid arguments for the PUT, checking preconditions does not affect the PUT's execution time much. Also, checking preconditions with RAC will improve the execution time of PUTs that catch an internally thrown exception during execution, because when the precondition is violated, the PUT is not run at all.

4   Experimental Study

To determine if our approach is practical, we compare JMLKelinci with standard Kelinci, measuring[2]: (1) the percentage of branches covered with valid inputs and (2) the time taken to achieve 100% branch coverage. We measured validity using JML's RAC and used JaCoCo [28] to measure the percentage of branches covered with valid inputs.

The programs tested were 28 (correct) programs annotated with JML preconditions from the Java+JML dataset [31,51]. Although this dataset's programs are small, it was chosen because it already has JML specifications, and we also wanted to extend our study to detecting semantic bugs with postconditions. In this study, the same initial seed input was used for Kelinci and JMLKelinci,

---

[2] Our study used an Intel i7-3770 CPU @ 3.40 GHz with 15 GB of RAM.

which required us to find initial seeds that did not crash the program using standard Kelinci. Also, we did not use JML to specify the exceptional behavior of the program's entry method; that is, the precondition specified guaranteed that no exceptions were thrown.

In this study, both tools were run five times on each program, and the average execution time and covered branches are calculated.

Table 1. Nontrivial programs. "JK" stands for JMLKelinci and "K" stands for Kelinci.

Program name	Avg. JK Valid Coverage	Avg. JK Time (sec.)	Avg. K Valid Coverage	Avg. K Time (sec.)	Best K Valid Coverage
AddLoop	100%	26.8	36.6%	21	50%
BankAccount	100%	10606.2	99.5%	26181	100%
BinarySearch	100%	349.2	10%	119.6	10%
Calculator	100%	10720.8	76.6%	12681.8	83%
ComboPermut	100%	364.6	6.6%	949	33%
CopyArray	100%	8704.2	0%	10	0%
Factorial	100%	59.2	25%	179.6	25%
FindFirstSorted	100%	1110.2	6%	224.2	30%
FindInSorted	100%	1007.4	0%	5	0%
LeapYear	100%	32.2	89.8%	38.6	100%
Perimeter	100%	5730.4	8.6%	581.8	29%
PrimeCheck	100%	21	75%	5.2	75%
StudentEnroll	100%	98.2	83.3%	84.4	89.5%
Time	100%	8434.2	5.8%	19981	29.1%
Average	100%	3376	37.3%	4361.6	46.7%

Table 1 shows the results of 14 programs in the dataset that have nontrivial preconditions. In this table JK and K stand for JMLKelinci and standard Kelinci, respectively. The "Best K Valid Coverage" is the highest coverage achieved with valid inputs in one individual run of a program using standard Kelinci. Also, "Avg. K Valid Coverage" and "Avg. JK Valid Coverage" are the average branch coverage using valid inputs with Kelinci and JMLKelinci, respectively. The time and coverage averages of five runs for each individual program are rounded to one decimal point. Recall that branch coverage is based on normal behavior, excluding paths that throw exceptions.

The results in Table 1 show that tests generated by JMLKelinci, as expected, covered all branches with valid inputs in these 14 nontrivial programs. However, the tests generated by standard Kelinci did not cover all branches with valid inputs since we stopped a run of Kelinci when it reached 100% branch coverage, while some of the branches may be covered with invalid inputs. Results show that standard Kelinci, on average, covered about 37.3% of branches in these nontrivial programs with valid inputs. Also, the average of the maximum coverage with valid inputs achieved by standard Kelinci on each program was about 46.7%.

Among nontrivial programs, JMLKelinci covered branches with valid inputs about 22.5% faster than standard Kelinci covered branches (possibly with invalid inputs). However, standard Kelinci covered branches faster in nine programs (some branches covered with invalid inputs) than JMLKelinci. Also, in some programs, standard Kelinci covered branches much faster, like "BinarySearch," "FindInSorted" and "FindFirstSorted," because JMLKelinci enforces the precondition that a sorted array is needed as an input; thus, JMLKelinci must examine many generated inputs until it finds one representing a sorted array. In these examples, unsorted arrays generated by standard Kelinci covered all branches, even though they were not valid inputs. Also, in these three examples, less than 10% of branches were covered with valid inputs by standard Kelinci. However, in five programs like "Factorial," "CombinationPermutation" and "Time" JMLKelinci could cover branches with valid inputs around three times faster than standard Kelinci (which may use invalid inputs to cover branches). This is because the execution time of these three programs can be very high when generated inputs are invalid. Also, the range of valid inputs for these programs is small. For example, the range of inputs in "Factorial" is limited to zero to twenty to avoid (long) integer overflow, but such valid inputs also finish much more quickly.

Table 2. Trivial programs. "JK" stands for JMLKelinci and "K" stands for Kelinci.

Program name	Avg. JK Valid Coverage	Avg. JK Time (sec.)	Avg. K Valid Coverage	Avg. K Time (sec.)
Absolute	100%	6	100%	6
Alphabet	100%	20053.8	100%	13822.2
BubbleSort	100%	5	100%	5
Fibonacci	100%	155.6	100%	322.4
FindFirstZero	100%	765.6	100%	605.6
FindInArray	100%	5	100%	5
GCD	100%	1674.8	100%	2185.8
Inverse	100%	748.2	100%	650.8
LCM	100%	1524.6	100%	3558.4
LinearSearch	100%	16.2	100%	10.2
OddEven	100%	5	100%	5
Smallest	100%	400.6	100%	485.6
StrPalindrome	100%	5	100%	5
Transpose	100%	5	100%	5
Average	100%	1812.2	100%	1548

Table 2 indicates the results of 14 programs that have trivial preconditions. A program's precondition is trivial if it is true for almost all possible inputs. For example, "Absolute" is noted as having a trivial precondition since almost all integer inputs are valid (except the minimum Java integer value).

Results in Table 2 shows the "Avg. K Valid Coverage" and "Avg. JK Valid Coverage" that are the average branch coverage using valid inputs with Kelinci and JMLKelinci in five runs, respectively, are 100% for all trivial programs. Thus, both JMLKelinci and Kelinci covered all branches with valid inputs as was expected. On average, the time for covering all branches with standard Kelinci was about 14.5% faster than JMLKelinci, results are rounded to one decimal point. While in six programs, both covered branches simultaneously, and in four programs, JMLKelinci covered branches faster. In these programs, almost all inputs are valid. Thus the inputs generated by standard Kelinci are usually valid, and there are few invalid inputs to waste time. However, some programs, like "Fibonacci," in which all inputs are valid because the program throws an exception (caught internally) when an input is too large or too small. For such programs, JMLKelinci is about two times faster because we specified the JML preconditions to avoid the cases where exceptions would be thrown (and caught internally in the PUT).

We were also interested in whether our approach would help find semantic bugs. Thus, we also performed a preliminary study using a guided fuzzer and a RAC to check preconditions for discovering potential semantic bugs. We used 28 buggy programs from the BuggyJava+JML dataset [7,51], each the first version ("bug1") of a correct program. We ran JMLKelinci on these buggy programs, which provided a set of valid inputs for these programs that cover all branches. Then we tested these buggy programs with these valid inputs using JML's RAC to check pre- and postconditions. Our preliminary results show that using a RAC with a guided fuzzer effectively detects semantic bugs for 26 out of 28 buggy programs. JML's RAC did not find a semantic bug for "CombinationPermutation" and "FindFirstSorted" programs because the input test that covered the buggy branch worked correctly. In future work, we will expand this study by using postconditions automatically with all valid inputs generated by the guided fuzzer.

All experimental results for correct and buggy programs and the instruction for reproducing the JMLKelinci's experiments are available in a GitHub repository [50].

5   Conclusion

We described a technique for combining formal methods and a guided fuzzer by catching precondition violation exceptions thrown by the RAC and directing them down a single branch. Thus, JMLKelinci guarantees that the program under test is only given valid inputs. This technique is not limited to JML, Java, or Kelinci but can be applied to any language with a RAC and a guided fuzzer.

Our experiments show that JMLKelinci can cover all branches of programs with valid inputs, which does not happen with a (guided) fuzzer used by itself. In contrast, standard Kelinci covered some branches with invalid inputs in respect to the program precondition. Our preliminary study also shows that formal behavior specification using guided fuzzer tools can be used to discover semantic bugs by using pre- and postconditions.

Acknowledgement. Dr. Păsăreanu's work was partially funded by NSF Grant 1901136 (the HUGS project).

References

1. Ahrendt, W., Gladisch, C., Herda, M.: Proof-based test case generation. Deductive Software Verification – The KeY Book. LNCS, vol. 10001, pp. 415–451. Springer, Cham (2016). https://doi.org/10.1007/978-3-319-49812-6_12
2. Artho, C., et al.: Combining test case generation and runtime verification. Theor. Comput. Sci. **336**(2–3), 209–234 (2005)
3. Banks, G., Cova, M., Felmetsger, V., Almeroth, K., Kemmerer, R., Vigna, G.: SNOOZE: toward a Stateful NetwOrk prOtocol fuzZEr. In: Katsikas, S.K., López, J., Backes, M., Gritzalis, S., Preneel, B. (eds.) ISC 2006. LNCS, vol. 4176, pp. 343–358. Springer, Heidelberg (2006). https://doi.org/10.1007/11836810_25
4. Bardin, S., Kosmatov, N., Marre, B., Mentré, D., Williams, N.: Test case generation with PATHCRAWLER/LTEST: how to automate an industrial testing process. In: Margaria, T., Steffen, B. (eds.) ISoLA 2018. LNCS, vol. 11247, pp. 104–120. Springer, Cham (2018). https://doi.org/10.1007/978-3-030-03427-6_12
5. Boyapati, C., Khurshid, S., Marinov, D.: Korat: automated testing based on Java predicates. ACM SIGSOFT Softw. Eng. Notes **27**(4), 123–133 (2002)
6. Brucker, A.D., Wolff, B.: Symbolic test case generation for primitive recursive functions. In: Grabowski, J., Nielsen, B. (eds.) FATES 2004. LNCS, vol. 3395, pp. 16–32. Springer, Heidelberg (2005). https://doi.org/10.1007/978-3-540-31848-4_2
7. BuggyJavaJML. https://github.com/Amirfarhad-Nilizadeh/BuggyJavaJML. Accessed 05 May 2021
8. Bürdek, J., et al.: Facilitating reuse in multi-goal test-suite generation for software product lines. In: Egyed, A., Schaefer, I. (eds.) FASE 2015. LNCS, vol. 9033, pp. 84–99. Springer, Heidelberg (2015). https://doi.org/10.1007/978-3-662-46675-9_6
9. Burdy, L., et al.: An overview of JML tools and applications. Int. J. Softw. Tools Technol. Transfer **7**(3), 212–232 (2005). https://doi.org/10.1007/s10009-004-0167-4
10. Cadar, C., et al.: Symbolic execution for software testing in practice: preliminary assessment. In: 2011 33rd International Conference on Software Engineering (ICSE), pp. 1066–1071. IEEE (2011)
11. Cha, S.K., Avgerinos, T., Rebert, A., Brumley, D.: Unleashing mayhem on binary code. In: 2012 IEEE Symposium on Security and Privacy, pp. 380–394. IEEE (2012)
12. Chalin, P., Kiniry, J.R., Leavens, G.T., Poll, E.: Beyond assertions: advanced specification and verification with JML and ESC/Java2. In: de Boer, F.S., Bonsangue, M.M., Graf, S., de Roever, W.-P. (eds.) FMCO 2005. LNCS, vol. 4111, pp. 342–363. Springer, Heidelberg (2006). https://doi.org/10.1007/11804192_16

13. Cheon, Y., Leavens, G.T.: A simple and practical approach to unit testing: the JML and JUnit way. In: Magnusson, B. (ed.) ECOOP 2002. LNCS, vol. 2374, pp. 231–255. Springer, Heidelberg (2002). https://doi.org/10.1007/3-540-47993-7_10
14. Cheon, Y., Leavens, G.T.: The JML and JUnit way of unit testing and its implementation. Technical report TR# 04–02a, Department of Computer Science (2004)
15. Clarke, L.A., Rosenblum, D.S.: A historical perspective on runtime assertion checking in software development. ACM SIGSOFT Softw. Eng. Notes **31**(3), 25–37 (2006)
16. Cok, D.R.: Improved usability and performance of SMT solvers for debugging specifications. Int. J. Softw. Tools Technol. Transfer **12**(6), 467–481 (2010). https://doi.org/10.1007/s10009-010-0138-x
17. Cok, D.R.: OpenJML: JML for Java 7 by extending OpenJDK. In: Bobaru, M., Havelund, K., Holzmann, G.J., Joshi, R. (eds.) NFM 2011. LNCS, vol. 6617, pp. 472–479. Springer, Heidelberg (2011). https://doi.org/10.1007/978-3-642-20398-5_35
18. Corina, J., et al.: DIFUZE: interface aware fuzzing for kernel drivers. In: Proceedings of the 2017 ACM SIGSAC Conference on Computer and Communications Security, pp. 2123–2138 (2017)
19. Ernst, M.D., et al.: The Daikon system for dynamic detection of likely invariants. Sci. Comput. Program. **69**(1–3), 35–45 (2007)
20. Fraser, G., Arcuri, A.: EvoSuite: automatic test suite generation for object-oriented software. In: Proceedings of the 19th ACM SIGSOFT Symposium and the 13th European Conference on Foundations of Software Engineering, pp. 416–419 (2011)
21. Fraser, G., Arcuri, A.: EvoSuite: on the challenges of test case generation in the real world. In: 2013 IEEE Sixth International Conference on Software Testing, Verification and Validation, pp. 362–369. IEEE (2013)
22. Fraser, G., Arcuri, A.: A large-scale evaluation of automated unit test generation using evosuite. ACM Trans. Softw. Eng. Methodol. (TOSEM) **24**(2), 1–42 (2014)
23. Gligoric, M., Gvero, T., Jagannath, V., Khurshid, S., Kuncak, V., Marinov, D.: Test generation through programming in UDITA. In: Proceedings of the 32nd ACM/IEEE International Conference on Software Engineering, vol. 1, pp. 225–234 (2010)
24. Godefroid, P., Klarlund, N., Sen, K.: DART: directed automated random testing. In: Proceedings of the 2005 ACM SIGPLAN Conference on Programming Language Design and Implementation, pp. 213–223 (2005)
25. Godefroid, P., Peleg, H., Singh, R.: Learn&Fuzz: machine learning for input fuzzing. In: 2017 32nd IEEE/ACM International Conference on Automated Software Engineering (ASE), pp. 50–59. IEEE (2017)
26. Groce, A., Pinto, J.: A little language for testing. In: Havelund, K., Holzmann, G., Joshi, R. (eds.) NFM 2015. LNCS, vol. 9058, pp. 204–218. Springer, Cham (2015). https://doi.org/10.1007/978-3-319-17524-9_15
27. Groce, A., Pinto, J., Azimi, P., Mittal, P.: TSTL: a language and tool for testing. In: Proceedings of the 2015 International Symposium on Software Testing and Analysis, pp. 414–417 (2015)
28. Hoffmann, M.R., Mandrikov, E., Friedenhagen, M.: Java Code Coverage for Eclipse. https://www.eclemma.org/jacoco/. Accessed 05 May 2021
29. Holmes, J., et al.: TSTL: the template scripting testing language. Int. J. Softw. Tools Technol. Transfer **20**(1), 57–78 (2016). https://doi.org/10.1007/s10009-016-0445-y
30. Google Inc., et al.: Google/syzkaller. https://github.com/google/syzkaller. Accessed 05 May 2021

31. Java-JML. https://github.com/Amirfarhad-Nilizadeh/Java-JML. Accessed 05 May 2021
32. Johansson, W., Svensson, M., Larson, U.E., Almgren, M., Gulisano, V.: T-Fuzz: model-based fuzzing for robustness testing of telecommunication protocols. In: 2014 IEEE Seventh International Conference on Software Testing, Verification and Validation, pp. 323–332. IEEE (2014)
33. Kersten, R., Luckow, K., Păsăreanu, C.S.: POSTER: AFL-based fuzzing for Java with Kelinci. In: Proceedings of the 2017 ACM SIGSAC Conference on Computer and Communications Security, pp. 2511–2513 (2017)
34. Kosmatov, N., Maurica, F., Signoles, J.: Efficient runtime assertion checking for properties over mathematical numbers. In: Deshmukh, J., Ničković, D. (eds.) RV 2020. LNCS, vol. 12399, pp. 310–322. Springer, Cham (2020). https://doi.org/10.1007/978-3-030-60508-7_17
35. Kwong, G., Ruderman, J., Carette, A.: MozillaSecurity/funfuzz. https://github.com/MozillaSecurity/funfuzz. Accessed 05 May 2021
36. Le, X.B.D., Pasareanu, C., Padhye, R., Lo, D., Visser, W., Sen, K.: SAFFRON: adaptive grammar-based fuzzing for worst-case analysis. ACM SIGSOFT Softw. Eng. Notes **44**(4), 14–14 (2019)
37. Leavens, G.T., Baker, A.L., Ruby, C.: JML: a notation for detailed design. In: Kilov, H., Rumpe, B., Simmonds, I. (eds.) Behavioral Specifications of Businesses and Systems. SECS, vol. 523, pp. 175–188. Springer, Boston (1999). https://doi.org/10.1007/978-1-4615-5229-1_12
38. Leavens, G.T., Baker, A.L., Ruby, C.: Preliminary design of JML: a behavioral interface specification language for Java. ACM SIGSOFT Softw. Eng. Notes **31**(3), 1–38 (2006)
39. Leavens, G.T., Cheon, Y.: Design by contract with JML (2006). https://www.cs.ucf.edu/~leavens/JML//jmldbc.pdf
40. Leavens, G.T., Cheon, Y., Clifton, C., Ruby, C., Cok, D.R.: How the design of JML accommodates both runtime assertion checking and formal verification. Sci. Comput. Program. **55**(1–3), 185–208 (2005)
41. Leavens, G.T., Ruby, C., Leino, K.R.M., Poll, E., Jacobs, B.: JML (poster session) notations and tools supporting detailed design in JAVA. In: Addendum to the 2000 Proceedings of the Conference on Object-Oriented Programming, Systems, Languages, and Applications (Addendum), pp. 105–106 (2000)
42. Leucker, M., Schallhart, C.: A brief account of runtime verification. J. Log. Algebraic Program. **78**(5), 293–303 (2009)
43. Li, J., Zhao, B., Zhang, C.: Fuzzing: a survey. Cybersecurity **1**(1) (2018). Article number: 6. https://doi.org/10.1186/s42400-018-0002-y
44. Liang, H., Pei, X., Jia, X., Shen, W., Zhang, J.: Fuzzing: state of the art. IEEE Trans. Reliab. **67**(3), 1199–1218 (2018)
45. Ly, D., Kosmatov, N., Loulergue, F., Signoles, J.: Verified runtime assertion checking for memory properties. In: Ahrendt, W., Wehrheim, H. (eds.) TAP 2020. LNCS, vol. 12165, pp. 100–121. Springer, Cham (2020). https://doi.org/10.1007/978-3-030-50995-8_6
46. Meinke, K., Sindhu, M.A.: LBTest: a learning-based testing tool for reactive systems. In: 2013 IEEE Sixth International Conference on Software Testing, Verification and Validation, pp. 447–454. IEEE (2013)
47. Milicevic, A., Misailovic, S., Marinov, D., Khurshid, S.: Korat: a tool for generating structurally complex test inputs. In: 29th International Conference on Software Engineering (ICSE 2007), pp. 771–774. IEEE (2007)

48. Nagy, S., Hicks, M.: Full-speed fuzzing: reducing fuzzing overhead through coverage-guided tracing. In: 2019 IEEE Symposium on Security and Privacy (SP), pp. 787–802. IEEE (2019)

49. Nguyen, H.A., Dyer, R., Nguyen, T.N., Rajan, H.: Mining preconditions of APIs in large-scale code corpus. In: Proceedings of the 22nd ACM SIGSOFT International Symposium on Foundations of Software Engineering, pp. 166–177 (2014)

50. Nilizadeh, A.: JMLKelinci. http://github.com/Amirfarhad-Nilizadeh/JMLKelinci. Accessed 05 May 2021

51. Nilizadeh, A., Leavens, G., Le, X.B., Pasareanu, C., Cok, D.: Exploring true test overfitting in dynamic automated program repair using formal methods. In: 2021 14th IEEE Conference on Software Testing, Validation and Verification (ICST). IEEE (2021)

52. Nilizadeh, S., Noller, Y., Pasareanu, C.S.: DiffFuzz: differential fuzzing for side-channel analysis. In: 2019 IEEE/ACM 41st International Conference on Software Engineering (ICSE), pp. 176–187. IEEE (2019)

53. Noller, Y., Kersten, R., Păsăreanu, C.S.: Badger: complexity analysis with fuzzing and symbolic execution. In: Proceedings of the 27th ACM SIGSOFT International Symposium on Software Testing and Analysis, pp. 322–332 (2018)

54. Pacheco, C., Ernst, M.D.: Randoop: feedback-directed random testing for Java. In: Companion to the 22nd ACM SIGPLAN Conference on Object-Oriented Programming Systems and Applications Companion, pp. 815–816 (2007)

55. Pacheco, C., Lahiri, S.K., Ernst, M.D., Ball, T.: Feedback-directed random test generation. In: 29th International Conference on Software Engineering (ICSE 2007), pp. 75–84. IEEE (2007)

56. Peters, D., Parnas, D.L.: Generating a test oracle from program documentation: work in progress. In: Proceedings of the 1994 ACM SIGSOFT International Symposium on Software Testing and Analysis, pp. 58–65 (1994)

57. Rajpal, M., Blum, W., Singh, R.: Not all bytes are equal: neural byte sieve for fuzzing. arXiv preprint arXiv:1711.04596 (2017)

58. Rawat, S., Jain, V., Kumar, A., Cojocar, L., Giuffrida, C., Bos, H.: VUzzer: application-aware evolutionary fuzzing. In: NDSS, vol. 17, pp. 1–14 (2017)

59. Stephens, N., et al.: Driller: augmenting fuzzing through selective symbolic execution. In: NDSS, vol. 16, pp. 1–16 (2016)

60. Visser, W., Geldenhuys, J.: COASTAL: combining concolic and fuzzing for Java (competition contribution). In: Biere, A., Parker, D. (eds.) TACAS 2020. LNCS, vol. 12079, pp. 373–377. Springer, Cham (2020). https://doi.org/10.1007/978-3-030-45237-7_23

61. Visser, W., Păsăreanu, C.S., Khurshid, S.: Test input generation with Java pathfinder. In: Proceedings of the 2004 ACM SIGSOFT International Symposium on Software Testing and Analysis, pp. 97–107 (2004)

62. Wang, T., Wei, T., Gu, G., Zou, W.: TaintScope: a checksum-aware directed fuzzing tool for automatic software vulnerability detection. In: 2010 IEEE Symposium on Security and Privacy, pp. 497–512. IEEE (2010)

63. Wang, X., Hu, C., Ma, R., Li, B., Wang, X.: LAFuzz: neural network for efficient fuzzing. In: 2020 IEEE 32nd International Conference on Tools with Artificial Intelligence (ICTAI), pp. 603–611. IEEE (2020)

64. Xu, G., Yang, Z.: JMLAutoTest: a novel automated testing framework based on JML and JUnit. In: Petrenko, A., Ulrich, A. (eds.) FATES 2003. LNCS, vol. 2931, pp. 70–85. Springer, Heidelberg (2004). https://doi.org/10.1007/978-3-540-24617-6_6

65. Yue, T., Tang, Y., Yu, B., Wang, P., Wang, E.: LearnAFL: greybox fuzzing with knowledge enhancement. IEEE Access **7**, 117029–117043 (2019)
66. Zalewski, M.: Technical "whitepaper" for afl-fuzz (2014). http://lcamtuf.coredump. cx/afl/technical_details.txt
67. Zimmerman, D.M., Nagmoti, R.: JMLUnit: the next generation. In: Beckert, B., Marché, C. (eds.) FoVeOOS 2010. LNCS, vol. 6528, pp. 183–197. Springer, Heidelberg (2011). https://doi.org/10.1007/978-3-642-18070-5_13

FuSeBMC: An Energy-Efficient Test Generator for Finding Security Vulnerabilities in C Programs

Kaled M. Alshmrany[1,2]([⊠]) [iD], Mohannad Aldughaim[1] [iD],
Ahmed Bhayat[1] [iD], and Lucas C. Cordeiro[1] [iD]

[1] University of Manchester, Manchester, UK
kaled.alshmrany@postgrad.manchester.ac.uk
[2] Institute of Public Administration, Jeddah, Saudi Arabia

Abstract. We describe and evaluate a novel approach to automated test generation that exploits fuzzing and Bounded Model Checking (BMC) engines to detect security vulnerabilities in C programs. We implement this approach in a new tool *FuSeBMC* that explores and analyzes the target C program by injecting labels that guide the engines to produce test cases. *FuSeBMC* also exploits a selective fuzzer to produce test cases for the labels that fuzzing and BMC engines could not produce test cases. Lastly, we manage each engine's execution time to improve *FuSeBMC*'s energy consumption. We evaluate *FuSeBMC* by analysing the results of its participation in Test-Comp 2021 whose two main categories evaluate a tool's ability to provide *code coverage* and *bug detection*. The competition results show that *FuSeBMC* performs well compared to the state-of-the-art software testing tools. *FuSeBMC* achieved 3 awards in the Test-Comp 2021: first place in the *Cover-Error* category, second place in the *Overall* category, and third place in the *Low Energy Consumption* category.

Keywords: Automated test generation · Bounded model checking · Fuzzing · Security

1 Introduction

Developing software that is secure and bug-free is an extraordinarily challenging task. Due to the devastating effects vulnerabilities may have, financially or on an individual's well-being, software verification is a necessity [1]. For example, Airbus found a software vulnerability in the A400M aircraft that caused a crash in 2015. This vulnerability created a fault in the control units for the engines, which caused them to power off shortly after taking-off [2]. A software vulnerability is best described as a defect or weakness in software design [3]. That design can be verified by Model Checking [4] or Fuzzing [5]. Model-checking and fuzzing are two techniques that are well suited to find bugs. In particular,

F. Loulergue and F. Wotawa (Eds.): TAP 2021, LNCS 12740, pp. 85–105, 2021.
https://doi.org/10.1007/978-3-030-79379-1_6

model-checking has proven to be one of the most successful techniques based on its use in research and industry [6]. This paper will focus on fuzzing and bounded model checking (BMC) techniques for code coverage and vulnerability detection. Code coverage has proven to be a challenge due to the state space problem, where the search space to be explored becomes extremely large [6]. For example, vulnerabilities are hard to detect in network protocols because the state-space of sophisticated protocol software is too large to be explored [7]. Vulnerability detection is another challenge that we have to take besides the code coverage. Some vulnerabilities cannot be detected without going deep into the software implementation. Many reasons motivate us to verify software for coverage and to detect security vulnerabilities formally. Therefore, these problems have attracted many researchers' attention to developing automated tools.

Researchers have been advancing the state-of-the-art to detect software vulnerabilities, as observed in the recent edition of the International Competition on Software Testing (Test-Comp 2021) [8]. Test-Comp is a competition that aims to reflect the state-of-the-art in software testing to the community and establish a set of benchmarks for software testing. Test-Comp 2021 [8], had two categories *Error Coverage* (or *Cover-Error*) and *Branch Coverage* (or *Cover-Branches*). The *Error Coverage* category tests the tool's ability to discover bugs where every C program in the benchmarks contains a bug. The aim of the *Branch Coverage* category is to cover as many program branches as possible. Test-Comp 2021 works as follows: each tool task is a pair of an input program (a program under test) and a test specification. The tool then should generate a test suite according to the test specification. A test suite is a sequence of test cases, given as a directory of files according to the format for exchangeable test-suites[1]. The specification for testing a program is given to the test generator as an input file (either coverage-error-call.prp or coverage branches.prp for Test-Comp 2021) [8].

Techniques such as fuzzing [9], symbolic execution [10], static code analysis [11], and taint tracking [12] are the most common techniques, which were employed in Test-Comp 2021 to cover branches and detect security vulnerabilities [8]. Fuzzing is generally unable to create various inputs that exercise all paths in the software execution. Symbolic execution might also not achieve high path coverage because of the dependence on Satisfiability Modulo Theories (SMT) solvers and the path-explosion problem. Consequently, fuzzing and symbolic execution by themselves often cannot reach deep software states. In particular, the deep states' vulnerabilities cannot be identified and detected by these techniques in isolation [13]. Therefore, a hybrid technique involving fuzzing and symbolic execution might achieve better code coverage than fuzzing or symbolic execution alone. VeriFuzz [14] and LibKluzzer [15] are the most prominent tools that combine these techniques. VeriFuzz combines the power of feedback-driven evolutionary fuzz testing with static analysis, where LibKluzzer combines the strengths of coverage-guided fuzzing and dynamic symbolic execution.

This paper proposes a novel method for detecting security vulnerabilities in C programs that combines fuzzing with symbolic execution via bounded model

---

[1] https://gitlab.com/sosy-lab/software/test-format/.

checking. We make use of coverage-guided fuzzing to produce random inputs to locate security vulnerabilities in C programs. Separately, we make use of BMC techniques [16, 17]. BMC unfolds a program up to depth k by evaluating (conditional) branch sides and merging states after that branch. It builds one logical formula expressed in a fragment of first-order theories and checks the satisfiability of the resulting formula using SMT solvers. These two methods are combined in our tool *FuSeBMC* which can consequently handle the two main features in software testing: *bug detection* and *code coverage*, as defined by Beyer et al. [18]. We also manage each engine's execution time to improve *FuSeBMC*'s efficiency in terms of verification time. Therefore, we raise the chance of bug detection due to its ability to cover different blocks of the C program, which other tools could not reach, e.g., KLEE [19], CPAchecker [20], VeriFuzz [14], and LibKluzzer [15].

Contributions. This paper extends our prior work [21] by making the following original contributions.

– We detail how *FuSeBMC* guides fuzzing and BMC engines to produce test cases that can detect security vulnerabilities and achieve high code coverage while massively reducing the consumption of both CPU and memory. Furthermore, we discuss using a custom fuzzer we refer to as a *selective fuzzer* as a third engine that learns from the test cases produced by fuzzing/BMC to produce new test cases for the uncovered goals.
– We provide a detailed analysis of the results from *FuSeBMC*'s successful participation in Test-Comp 2021. *FuSeBMC* achieved first place in *Cover-Error* category and second place in *Overall* category. *FuSeBMC* achieved first place in the subcategories *ReachSafety-BitVectors*, *ReachSafety-Floats*, *ReachSafety-Recursive*, *ReachSafety-Sequentialized* and *ReachSafety-XCSP*. We analyse the results in depth and explain how our research has enabled *FuSeBMC*'s success across these categories as well its low energy consumption.

2 Preliminaries

2.1 Fuzzing

Fuzzing is a cost-effective software testing technique to exploit vulnerabilities in software systems [22]. The basic idea is to generate random inputs and check whether an application crashes; it is not testing functional correctness (compliance). Critical security flaws most often occur because program inputs are not adequately checked [23]. Therefore, fuzzing prepares random or semi-random inputs, which might consider, e.g., (1) very long or completely blank strings; (2) min/max values of integers, or only zero and negative values; and (3) include unique values or characters likely to trigger bugs. Software systems that cannot endure fuzzing could potentially lead to security holes. For example, a bug was found in Apple wireless driver by utilizing file system fuzzing. The driver could not handle some beacon frames, which led to out-of-bounds memory access.

2.2   Symbolic Execution

Introduced in the 1970s, symbolic execution [24] is a software analysis technique that allowed developers to test specific properties in their software. The main idea is to execute a program symbolically using a symbolic execution engine that keeps track of every path the program may take for every input [24]. Moreover, each input represents symbolic input values instead of concrete input values. This method treats the paths as symbolic constraints and solves the constraints to output a concrete input as a test case. Symbolic execution is widely used to find security vulnerabilities by analyzing program behavior and generating test cases [25]. BMC is an instance of symbolic execution, where it merges all execution paths into one single logical formula instead of exploring them individually.

2.3   Types of Vulnerabilities

Software, in general, is prone to vulnerabilities caused by developer errors, which include: *buffer overflow*, where a running program attempts to write data outside the memory buffer, which is intended to store this data [26]; *memory leak*, which occurs when programmers create a memory in a heap and forget to delete it [27]; *integer overflows*, when the value of an integer is greater than the integer's maximum size in memory or less than the minimum value of an integer. It usually occurs when converting a signed integer to an unsigned integer and vice-versa [28]. Another example is *string manipulation*, where the string may contain malicious code and is accepted as an input; this is reasonably common in the C programming language [29]. *Denial-of-service attack* (DoS) is a security event that occurs when an attacker prevents legitimate users from accessing specific computer systems, devices, services, or other IT resources [30]. For example, a vulnerability in the Cisco Discovery Protocol (CDP) module of Cisco IOS XE Software Releases 16.6.1 and 16.6.2 could have allowed an unauthenticated, adjacent attacker to cause a memory leak, which could have lead to a DoS condition [31]. Part of our motivation is to mitigate the harm done by these vulnerabilities by the proposed method *FuSeBMC*.

3   *FuSeBMC*: An Energy-Efficient Test Generator for Finding Security Vulnerabilities in C Programs

We propose a novel verification method named *FuSeBMC* (cf. Fig. 1) for detecting security vulnerabilities in C programs using fuzzing and BMC techniques. *FuSeBMC* builds on top of the Clang compiler [32] to instrument the C program, uses Map2check [33,34] as a fuzzing engine, and ESBMC (Efficient SMT-based Bounded Model Checker) [35,36] as BMC and symbolic execution engines, thus combining dynamic and static verification techniques.

The method proceeds as follows. First, *FuSeBMC* takes a C program and a test specification as input. Then, *FuSeBMC* invokes the fuzzing and BMC engines sequentially to find an execution path that violates a given property.

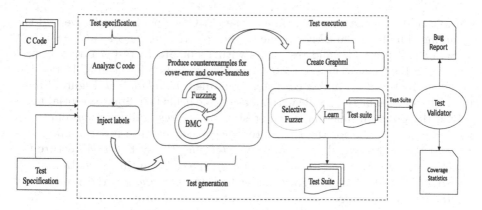

Fig. 1. *FuSeBMC*: an energy-efficient test generator framework.

It uses an iterative BMC approach that incrementally unwinds the program until it finds a property violation or exhausts time or memory limits. In code coverage mode, *FuSeBMC* explores and analyzes the target C program using the clang compiler to inject labels incrementally. *FuSeBMC* traverses every branch of the Clang AST and injects a label in each of the form $GOAL_i$ for $i \in \mathbb{N}$. Then, both engines will check whether these injected labels are reachable to produce test cases for branch coverage. After that, *FuSeBMC* analyzes the counterexamples and saves them as a *graphml* file. It checks whether the fuzzing and BMC engines could produce counterexamples for both categories *Cover-Error* and *Cover-Branches*. If that is not the case, FuSeBMC employs a second fuzzing engine, the so-called selective fuzzer (cf. Sect. 3.6), which attempts to produce test cases for the rest of the labels. The selective fuzzer produces test cases by learning from the two previous engines' output.

FuSeBMC introduces a novel algorithm for managing the time allocated to its component engines. In particular, *FuSeBMC* manages the time allocated to each engine to avoid wasting time for a specific engine to find test cases for challenging goals. For example, let us assume we have 100 goals injected by *FuSeBMC* and1000 s to produce test cases. In this case, *FuSeBMC* distributes the time per engine per goal so that each goal will have 10s and recalculate the time for the goals remaining after each goal passed. If an engine succeeds on a particular goal within the time limit, the extra time is redistributed to the other goals; otherwise, *FuSeBMC* kills the process that passes the time set for it.

Furthermore, *FuSeBMC* has a minimum time, which a goal must be allocated. If there are too many goals for all to receive this minimum time, *FuSeBMC* will select a subset to attempt using a quasi-random strategy (e.g., all even-numbered goals). *FuSeBMC* also manages the global time of the fuzzing, BMC, and selective fuzzing engines. It gives 13% of the time for fuzzing, 77% for BMC, and 10% for selective fuzzing. *FuSeBMC* further carries out time management at this global level to maximize engine usage. If, for example, the fuzzing engine is finished before the time allocated to it, its remaining time will be carried over and added to the allocated time of the BMC engine. Similarly, we add the remaining time from the BMC engine to the selective fuzzer allocated time.

FuSeBMC prepares valid test cases with metadata to test a target C program using TestCov [37] as a test validator. The metadata file is an XML file that describes the test suite and is consistently named *metadata.xml*. Figure 2 illustrates an example metadata file with all available fields [37]. Some essential fields include the program function that is tested by the test suite $\langle entryfunction \rangle$, the coverage criterion for the test suite $\langle specification \rangle$, the programming language of the program under test $\langle sourcecodelang \rangle$, the system architecture the program tests were created for $\langle architecture \rangle$, the creation time $\langle creationtime \rangle$, the SHA-256 hash of the program under test $\langle programhash \rangle$, the producer of counterexample $\langle producer \rangle$ and the name of the target program $\langle programfile \rangle$. A test case file contains a sequence of tags $\langle input \rangle$ that describes the input values sequence. Figure 3 illustrates an example of the test case file.

Algorithm 1 describes the main steps we implemented in *FuSeBMC*. It consists of extracting all *goals* of a C program (line 1). For each goal, the instrumented C program, containing the goals (line 2), is executed on our verification engines (fuzzing and BMC) to check the reachability property produced by REACH(G) for that goal (lines 8 & 20). REACH is a function; it takes a goal (G) as input and produces a corresponding property for fuzzing/BMC (line 7 & 19). If our engines find that the property is violated, meaning that there is a valid execution path that reaches the goal (counterexample), then the goals are marked as covered, and the test case is saved for later (lines 9–11). Then, we continue if we still have time allotted for each engine. Otherwise, if our verification engines could not reach some goals, then we employ the selective fuzzer in attempt to reach these as yet uncovered goals. In the end, we return all test cases for all the goals we have found in the specified XML format (line 41).

```
1   <?xml version='1.0'>
2   <!DOCTYPE test-metadata PUBLIC [...]>
3   <test-metadata>
4     <entryfunction>main</entryfunction>
5     <specification>COVER(init(main()), FQL(COVER EDGES(@DECISIONEDGE)))
6       </specification>
7     <sourcecodelang>C</sourcecodelang>
8     <architecture>32bit</architecture>
9     <creationtime>2021-02-28 20:44:56.117416</creationtime>
10    <programhash>e8f2cf545726d8f791bfc137e9eca7e9de4cb696</programhash>
11    <producer>FuSeBMC</producer>
12    <programfile>sv-benchmarks/c/array-tiling/skippedu.c</programfile>
13  </test-metadata>
```

Fig. 2. An example of a metadata.

3.1   Analyze C Code

FuSeBMC explores and analyzes the target C programs as the first step using Clang [38]. In this phase, *FuSeBMC* analyzes every single line in the C code and considers the conditional statements such as the *if*-conditions, *for*, *while*,

---

Algorithm 1. Proposed *FuSeBMC* algorithm.

Require: program P
1: $goals \leftarrow clang\_extract\_goals(P)$
2: $instrumentedP \leftarrow clang\_instrument\_goals(P, goals)$
3: $reached\_goals \leftarrow \emptyset$
4: $tests \leftarrow \emptyset$
5: $FuzzingTime = 150$
6: **for all** $G \in goals$ **do**
7:     $\phi \leftarrow REACH(G)$
8:     $result, test\_case \leftarrow Fuzzing(instrumentedP, \phi, FuzzingTime)$
9:     **if** $result = false$ **then**
10:         $reached\_goals \leftarrow reached\_goals \cup G$
11:         $tests \leftarrow tests \cup test\_case$
12:     **end if**
13:     **if** $FuzzingTime = 0$ **then**
14:         $break$
15:     **end if**
16: **end for**
17: $BMCTime = FuzzingTime + 700$
18: **for all** $G \in (goals - reached\_goals)$ **do**
19:     $\phi \leftarrow REACH(G)$
20:     $result, test\_case \leftarrow BMC(instrumentedP, \phi, BMCTime)$
21:     **if** $result = false$ **then**
22:         $reached\_goals \leftarrow reached\_goals \cup G$
23:         $tests \leftarrow tests \cup test\_case$
24:     **end if**
25:     **if** $BMCTime = 0$ **then**
26:         $break$
27:     **end if**
28: **end for**
29: $SelectiveFuzzerTime = BMCTime + 50$
30: **for all** $G \in (goals - reached\_goals)$ **do**
31:     $\phi \leftarrow REACH(G)$
32:     $result \leftarrow selectivefuzzer(instrumentedP, \phi, SelectiveFuzzerTime)$
33:     **if** $result = false$ **then**
34:         $reached\_goals \leftarrow reached\_goals \cup G$
35:         $tests \leftarrow tests \cup test\_case$
36:     **end if**
37:     **if** $SelectiveFuzzerTime = 0$ **then**
38:         $break$
39:     **end if**
40: **end for**
41: **return** $tests$

---

and *do while* loops in the code. *FuSeBMC* takes all these branches as path conditions, containing different values due to the conditions set used to produce the counterexamples, thus helping increase the code coverage. It supports blocks, branches, and conditions. All the values of the variables within each path are

```
 1  <?xml version="1.0"?>
 2  <!DOCTYPE testcase PUBLIC [...]>
 3  <testcase>
 4    <input>2</input>
 5    <input>1</input>
 6    <input>128</input>
 7    <input>0</input>
 8    <input>0</input>
 9    <input>1</input>
10    <input>64</input>
11    <input>0</input>
12    <input>0</input>
13  </testcase>
```

Fig. 3. An example of test case file.

taken into account. Parentheses and the *else*-branch are added to compile the target code without errors.

3.2 Inject Labels

FuSeBMC injects labels of the form $GOAL_i$ in every branch in the C code as the second step. In particular, *FuSeBMC* adds *else* to the C code that has an *if*-condition with no *else* at the end of the condition. Additionally, *FuSeBMC* will consider this as another branch that should produce a counterexample for it to increase the chance of detecting bugs and covering more statements in the program. For example, the code in Fig. 4 consists of two branches: the *if*-branch is entered if condition $x < 0$ holds; otherwise, the *else*-branch is entered implicitly, which can exercise the remaining execution paths. Also, Fig. 4 shows how *FuSeBMC* injects the labels and considers it as a new branch.

```
1  #include <stdio.h>
2  int example () {
3      int x;
4      if ( x < 0 ){
5          //...
6      }
7  }
```

(a) Original C code.

```
 1  #include <stdio.h>
 2  int example () {
 3      int x;
 4      if ( x < 0 ){
 5          GOAL_1:;
 6          //...
 7      }
 8      else{
 9          GOAL_2:;
10      }
11      return 0;
12  }
```

(b) Code instrumented.

Fig. 4. Original C code vs code instrumented.

3.3 Produce Counterexamples

FuSeBMC uses its verification engines to generate test cases that can reach goals amongst $GOAL_1$, $GOAL_2$, ..., $GOAL_n$ inserted in the previous phase.

FuSeBMC then checks whether all goals within the C program are covered. If so, *FuSeBMC* continues to the next phase; otherwise, *FuSeBMC* passes the goals that are not covered to the selective fuzzer to produce test cases for it using randomly generated inputs learned from the test cases produced from both engines. Figure 5 illustrates how the method works.

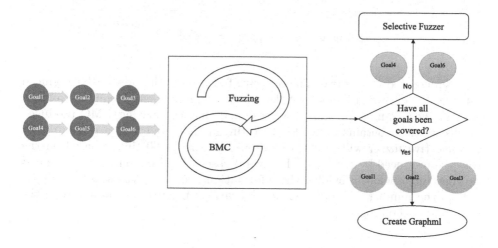

Fig. 5. Produce counterexamples.

3.4 Create Graphml

FuSeBMC will generate a *graphml* for each goal injected and then name it. The name of the *graphml* takes the number of the goal extended by the *graphml* extension, e.g., (*GOAL1.graphml*). The *graphml* file contains data about the counterexample, such as data types, values, and line numbers for the variables, which will be used to obtain the values of the target variable.

3.5 Produce Test Cases

In this phase, *FuSeBMC* will analyze all the *graphml* files produced in the previous phase. Practically, *FuSeBMC* will focus on the `<edge>` tags in the *graphml* that refer to the variable with a type non-deterministic. These variables will store their value in a file called, for example, (*testcase1.xml*). Figure 6 illustrates the edges and values used to create the test cases.

3.6 Selective Fuzzer

In this phase, we apply the selective fuzzer to learn from the test cases produced by either fuzzing or BMC engines to produce test cases for the goals that have

```
1    <edge id="E2" source="N2" target="N3">
2        <data key="startline">3</data>
3        <data key="assumption"> a = -2147483647;</data>
4        <data key="threadId">0</data>
5    </edge>
6
7    <edge id="E4" source="N4" target="N5">
8        <data key="startline">4</data>
9        <data key="assumption">b = 0;</data>
10       <data key="threadId">0</data>
11   </edge>
```

Fig. 6. An example of target edges

not been covered by the two. The selective fuzzer uses the previously produced test cases by extracting from each the number of assignments required to reach an error. For example, in Fig. 7, we assumed that the fuzzing/BMC produced a test case that contains values 18 (1000 times) generated from a random seed. The selective fuzzer will produce random numbers (1000 times) based on the test case produced by the fuzzer. In several cases, the BMC engine can exhaust the time limit before providing the information needed by the selective fuzzer, such as the number of inputs, when large arrays need to be initialized at the beginning of the program.

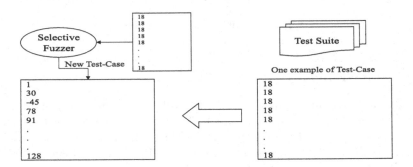

Fig. 7. The selective fuzzer

3.7   Test Validator

The test validator takes as input the test cases produced by *FuSeBMC* and then validates these test cases by executing the program on all test cases. The test validator checks whether the bug is exposed if the test was bug-detection, and it reports the code coverage if the test was a measure of the coverage. In our experiments, we use the tool TESTCOV [37] as a test validator. The tool provides coverage statistics per test. It supports block, branch, and condition coverage and covering calls to an error function. TESTCOV uses the XML-based exchange format for test cases specifications defined by Test-Comp [16].

TESTCOV was successfully used in recent editions of Test-Comp 2019, 2020, and 2021 to execute almost 9 million tests on 1720 different programs [37].

4 Evaluation

4.1 Description of Benchmarks and Setup

We conducted experiments with *FuSeBMC* on the benchmarks of Test-Comp 2021 [39] to check the tool's ability in the previously mentioned criteria. Our evaluation benchmarks are taken from the largest and most diverse open-source repository of software verification tasks. The same benchmark collection is used by SV-COMP [40]. These benchmarks yield 3173 test tasks, namely 607 test tasks for the category *Error Coverage* and 2566 test tasks for the category *Code Coverage*. Both categories contain C programs with loops, arrays, bit-vectors, floating-point numbers, dynamic memory allocation, and recursive functions.

The experiments were conducted on the server of Test-Comp 2021 [39]. Each run was limited to 8 processing units, 15 GB of memory, and 15 min of CPU time. The test suite validation was limited to 2 processing units, 7 GB of memory, and 5 min of CPU time. Also, the machine had the following specification of the test node was: one Intel Xeon E3-1230 v5 CPU, with 8 processing units each, a frequency of 3.4 GHz, 33 GB of RAM, and a GNU/Linux operating system (x86-64-Linux, Ubuntu 20.04 with Linux kernel 5.4).

FuSeBMC source code is written in C++; it is available for downloading at GitHub,[2] which includes the latest release of FuSeBMC v3.6.6. *FuSeBMC* is publicly available under the terms of the MIT license. Instructions for building *FuSeBMC* from the source code are given in the file *README.md*.

4.2 Objectives

This evaluation's main goal is to check the performance of *FuSeBMC* and the system's suitability for detecting security vulnerabilities in open-source C programs. Our experimental evaluation aims to answer three experimental goals:

EG1 **(Security Vulnerability Detection)** Can *FuSeBMC* generate test cases that lead to more security vulnerabilities than state-of-the-art software testing tools?

EG2 **(Coverage Capacity)** Can *FuSeBMC* achieve a higher coverage when compared with other state-of-the-art software testing tools?

EG3 **(Low Energy Consumption)** Can *FuSeBMC* reduce the consumption of CPU and memory compared with the state-of-the-art tools?

---

[2] https://github.com/kaled-alshmrany/FuSeBMC.

4.3 Results

First, we evaluated *FuSeBMC* on the *Error Coverage* category. Table 1 shows the experimental results compared with other tools in Test-Comp 2021 [39], where *FuSeBMC* achieved the 1st place in this category by solving 500 out of 607 tasks, an 82% success rate.

In detail, *FuSeBMC* achieved 1st place in the subcategories *ReachSafety-BitVectors, ReachSafety-Floats, ReachSafety-Recursive, ReachSafety-XCSP and ReachSafety-Sequentialized. FuSeBMC* solved 10 out of 10 tasks in *ReachSafety-BitVectors*, 32 out of 33 tasks in *ReachSafety-Floats*, 19 out of 20 tasks in *ReachSafety-Recursive*, 53 out of 59 tasks in *ReachSafety-XCSP* and 101 out of 107 tasks in *ReachSafety-Sequentialized*.

FuSeBMC outperformed the top tools in Test-Comp 2021, such as KLEE [19], CPAchecker [20], Symbiotic [41], LibKluzzer [15], and VeriFuzz [14] in these subcategories. However, *FuSeBMC* did not perform as well in the *ReachSafety-ECA* subcategory if compared with leading tools in the competition. We suspect that this is due to the prevalence of nested branches in these benchmarks. The *FuSeBMC*'s verification engines and the selective fuzzer could not produce test cases to reach the error due to the existence of too many path conditions, making the logical formula hard to solve and making it difficult to create random inputs to reach the error.

> Overall, the results show that *FuSeBMC* produces test cases that detect more security vulnerabilities in C programs than state-of-the-art tools, which successfully answers **EG1**.

FuSeBMC also participated in the *Branch Coverage* category at Test-Comp 2021. Table 2 shows the experimental results from this category. *FuSeBMC* achieved 4th place in the category by successfully achieving a score of 1161 out of 2566, behind the 3rd place system by 8 scores only. In the subcategory *ReachSafety-Floats*, *FuSeBMC* obtained the first place by achieving 103 out of 226 scores. Thus, *FuSeBMC* outperformed the top tools in Test-Comp 2021. Further, *FuSeBMC* obtained the first place in the subcategory *ReachSafety-XCSP* by achieving 97 out of 119 scores. However, *FuSeBMC* did not perform well in the subcategory *ReachSafety-ECA* compared with the leading tools in the Test-Comp 2021. Again we suspect the cause to be the prevalence of nested branches in these benchmarks.

> These results validate **EG2**. *FuSeBMC* proved its capability in *Branch Coverage* category, especially in the subcategories *ReachSafety-Floats and ReachSafety-XCSP*, where it ranked first.

FuSeBMC achieved 2nd place overall at Test-Comp 2021, with a score of 1776 out of 3173. Table 4 and Fig. 8 shows the overall results compared with other tools in the competition. Overall, *FuSeBMC* performed well compared

Table 1. *Cover-Error* results[a]. We identify the best for each tool in bold.

Cover-Error	Task-Num	FuSeBMC	CMA-ES Fuzz	CoVeriTest	HybridTiger	KLEE	Legion	LibKluzzer	PRTest	Symbiotic	Tracer-X	VeriFuzz
ReachSafety-Arrays	100	93	0	59	69	88	67	**96**	11	73	75	95
ReachSafety-BitVectors	10	**10**	0	8	6	9	0	9	5	8	7	9
ReachSafety-ControlFlow	32	8	0	8	8	10	0	**11**	0	7	9	9
ReachSafety-ECA	18	8	0	2	1	14	0	11	0	15	2	**16**
ReachSafety-Floats	33	**32**	0	16	22	6	0	30	3	0	0	30
ReachSafety-Heap	57	45	0	37	38	46	0	**47**	9	**47**	44	**47**
ReachSafety-Loops	158	131	0	35	53	96	4	**138**	102	82	78	136
ReachSafety-Recursive	20	**19**	0	0	5	16	0	17	1	17	14	13
ReachSafety-Sequentialized	107	**101**	0	61	93	86	0	83	0	79	57	99
ReachSafety-XCSP	59	**53**	0	46	52	37	0	3	0	41	31	25
SoftwareSystems-BusyBox-MemSafety	11	0	0	0	0	0	0	0	0	0	0	0
DeviceDriversLinux64-ReachSafety	2	0	0	0	0	0	0	0	0	0	0	0
Overall	607	**405**	0	225	266	339	35	359	79	314	246	385

[a] https://test-comp.sosy-lab.org/2021/results/results-verified/.

Table 2. *Cover-Branches* results[a]. We identify the best for each tool in bold.

Cover-Branches	Task-Num	FuSeBMC	CMA-ES Fuzz	CoVeriTest	HybridTiger	KLEE	Legion	LibKluzzer	PRTest	Symbiotic	Tracer-X	VeriFuzz
ReachSafety-Arrays	400	284	139	229	225	96	195	**296**	119	226	223	295
ReachSafety-BitVectors	62	37	23	39	13	28	29	**40**	27	37	37	38
ReachSafety-ControlFlow	67	15	4	16	3	8	8	16	5	**18**	15	**18**
ReachSafety-ECA	29	5	0	6	2	7	3	10	2	10	7	**12**
ReachSafety-Floats	226	**103**	51	98	84	16	64	90	41	50	48	99
ReachSafety-Heap	143	88	19	79	74	81	69	**90**	40	84	86	86
ReachSafety-Loops	581	412	152	402	338	274	271	419	252	383	385	**424**
ReachSafety-Recursive	53	36	19	31	31	18	20	36	9	**38**	34	35
ReachSafety-Sequentialized	82	62	0	61	39	26	1	55	8	36	41	**71**
ReachSafety-XCSP	119	**97**	0	80	80	81	2	80	79	93	69	88
ReachSafety-Combinations	210	15	0	31	8	82	18	139	2	135	99	**180**
SoftwareSystems-BusyBox-MemSafety	72	1	0	5	4	6	0	6	4	7	4	**8**
DeviceDriversLinux64-ReachSafety	290	35	13	**60**	6	25	56	58	16	44	56	57
SoftwareSystemsSQLite-MemSafety	1	0	0	0	0	0	0	0	0	0	0	0
Termination-MainHeap	231	202	138	193	189	119	166	199	51	178	185	**204**
Overall	2566	1161	411	1128	860	784	651	1292	519	1169	1087	**1389**

[a] https://test-comp.sosy-lab.org/2021/results/results-verified/.

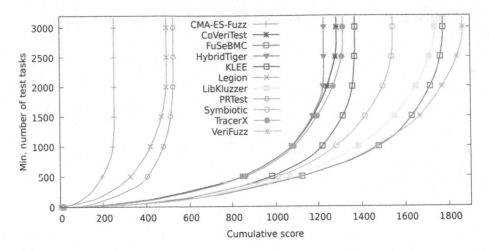

Fig. 8. Quantile functions for category *Overall*. [8]

Table 3. The consumption of CPU and memory [8].

Rank	Test generator	Quality (sp)	CPU time (h)	CPU Energy (kWh)	Rank measure
Green testing					(kj/sp)
1	TRACERX	1315	210	2.5	6.8
2	KLEE	1370	210	2.6	6.8
3	FuSeBMC	1776	410	4.8	9.7
Worst					51

with top tools in the subcategories *ReachSafety-BitVectors, ReachSafety-Floats, ReachSafety-Recursive, ReachSafety-Sequentialized and ReachSafety-XCSP.*

Test-Comp 2021 also considers energy efficiency in rankings since a large part of the cost of test generation is caused by energy consumption. *FuSeBMC* is classified as a Green-testing tool - Low Energy Consumption tool (see Table 3). *FuSeBMC* consumed less energy than many other tools in the competition. This ranking category uses the energy consumption per score point as a rank measure: CPU Energy Quality, with the unit kilo-joule per score point (kJ/sp). It uses CPU Energy Meter [42] for measuring the energy.

> These experimental results showed that *FuSeBMC* could reduce the consumption of CPU and memory efficiently and effectively in C programs, which answers **EG3**.

Table 4. Test-Comp 2021 *Overall* results[a].

Cover-Error and Branches	Task-Num	*FuSeBMC*	CMA-ES Fuzz	CoVeriTest	HybridTiger	KLEE	Legion	LibKluzzer	PRTest	Symbiotic	Tracer-X	VeriFuzz
OVERALL	3173	1776	254	1286	1228	1370	495	1738	526	1543	1315	**1865**

[a]https://test-comp.sosy-lab.org/2021/results/results-verified/.

5   Related Work

For more than 20 years, software vulnerabilities have been mainly identified by fuzzing [43]. American fuzzy lop (AFL) [44,45] is a tool that aims to find software vulnerabilities. AFL increases the coverage of test cases by utilizing genetic algorithms (GA) with guided fuzzing. Another fuzzing tool is LibFuzzer [46]. LibFuzzer generates test cases by using code coverage information provided by LLVM's Sanitizer Coverage instrumentation. It is best used for programs with small inputs that have a run-time of less than a fraction of a second for each input as it is guaranteed not to crash on invalid inputs. AutoFuzz [47] is a tool that verifies network protocols using fuzzing. First, it determines the specification for the protocol, then utilizes fuzzing to find vulnerabilities. Additionally, Peach [48] is an advanced and robust fuzzing framework that provides an XML file to create a data model and state model definition.

Symbolic execution has also been used to identify security vulnerabilities. One of the most popular symbolic execution engines is KLEE [19]. It is built on top of the LLVM compiler infrastructure and employs dynamic symbolic execution to explore the search space path-by-path. KLEE has proven to be a reliable symbolic execution engine for its utilization in many specialized tools such as TracerX [49] and Map2Check [33] for software verification, also SymbexNet [50] and SymNet [51] for verification of network protocols implementation.

The combination of symbolic execution and fuzzing has been proposed before. It started with the tool that earned first place in Test-Comp 2020 [18], Veri-Fuzz [14]. VeriFuzz is a state-of-the-art tool we have compared to *FuSeBMC*. It is a program-aware fuzz tester that combines the power of feedback-driven evolutionary fuzz testing with static analysis. It is built based on grey-box fuzzing to exploit lightweight instrumentation for observing the behaviors that occur during test runs. There is also LibKluzzer [15], which is a novel implementation that combines the strengths of coverage-guided fuzzing and white-box fuzzing. LibKluzzer is a combination of LibFuzzer and an extension of KLEE called KLUZZER [52]. Driller [53] is a hybrid vulnerability excavation tool, which leverages fuzzing and selective concolic execution in a complementary manner to find deeply embedded bugs. The authors avoid the path explosion inherent in concolic analysis and the incompleteness of fuzzing by combining the two techniques' strengths and mitigating the weaknesses. Driller splits the application into *compartments* based on checks of particular values of a specific input. The proficiency of fuzzing allows it to explore possible values of general input in a compartment. However, when it comes to values that satisfy checks on an input that guides the execution between *compartments*, fuzzing struggles to identify such values. In contrast, selective concolic execution excels at identifying such values required by checks and drive the execution between *compartments*.

Another example is hybrid fuzzer [54], which provides an efficient way to generate provably random test cases that guarantee the execution of unique paths. It uses symbolic execution to determine frontier nodes that lead to a unique execution path. Given some resource constraints, the tool collects as many frontier nodes as possible. With these nodes, fuzzing is employed with provably random input, preconditioned to lead to each frontier node. Badger [55] is a hybrid testing approach for complexity analysis. It uses Symbolic PathFinder [56] to generate new inputs and provides the Kelinci fuzzer with worst-case analysis. Munch [57] is a hybrid tool introduced to increase function coverage. It employs fuzzing with seed inputs generated by symbolic execution and targets symbolic execution when fuzzing saturates. SAGE (Scalable Automated Guided Execution) [58] is a hybrid fuzzer developed at Microsoft Research. It extends dynamic symbolic execution with a generational search; it negates and solves the path predicates to increase the code coverage. SAGE is used extensively at Microsoft, where it has been successful at finding many security-related bugs. SAFL [59] is an efficient fuzzer for C/C++ programs. It generates initial seeds that can get an appropriate fuzzing direction by employing symbolic execution in a lightweight approach. He et al. [60] describe a new approach for learning a fuzzer from symbolic execution; they instantiated it to the domain of smart contracts. First, it learns a fuzzing policy using neural networks. Then it generates inputs for fuzzing unseen smart contracts by this learning fuzzing policy. In summary, many tools have combined fuzzers with BMC and symbolic execution to perform software verification. However, our approach's novelty lies with the addition of the selective fuzzer and time management algorithm between engines and goals. These features were what distinguished *FuSeBMC* from other tools at Test-Comp 2021.

6   Conclusions and Future Work

We proposed a novel test case generation approach that combined Fuzzing and BMC and implemented it in the *FuSeBMC* tool. *FuSeBMC* explores and analyzes the target C programs by incrementally injecting labels to guide the fuzzing and BMC engines to produce test cases. We inject labels in every program branch to check for their reachability, producing test cases if these labels are reachable. We also exploit the selective fuzzer to produce test cases for the labels that fuzzing and BMC could not produce test cases. *FuSeBMC* achieved two significant awards from Test-Comp 2021. First place in the *Cover-Error* category and second place in the *Overall* category. *FuSeBMC* outperformed the leading state-of-the-art tools because of two main factors. Firstly, the usage of the selective fuzzer as a third engine that learns from the test cases of fuzzing/BMC to produce new test cases for the as-yet uncovered goals. Overall, it substantially increased the percentage of successful tasks. Secondly, we apply a novel algorithm of managing the time allocated for each engine and goal. This algorithm prevents *FuSeBMC* from wasting time finding test cases for difficult goals so that if the fuzzing engine is finished before the time allocated to it, the remaining time will be carried over and added to the allocated time of the BMC engine. Similarly, we add the remaining time from the BMC engine to the selective fuzzer allocated time. As a result, *FuSeBMC* raised the bar for the competition, thus advancing state-of-the-art software testing. Future work will investigate the extension of *FuSeBMC* to test multi-threaded programs [61,62] and reinforcement learning techniques to guide our selective fuzzer to find test cases that path-based fuzzing and BMC could not find.

A   Appendix

A.1   Artifact

We have set up a zenodo entry that contains the necessary materials to reproduce the results given in this paper: https://doi.org/10.5281/zenodo.4710599. Also, it contains instructions to run the tool.

A.2   Tool Availability

FuSeBMC contents are publicly available in our repository in GitHub under the terms of the MIT License. *FuSeBMC* provides, besides other files, a script called *fusebmc.py*. In order to run our *fusebmc.py* script, one must set the architecture (i.e., 32 or 64-bit), the competition strategy (i.e., k-induction, falsification, or incremental BMC), the property file path, and the benchmark path. *FuSeBMC* participated in the 3rd international competition, Test-Comp 21, and met all the requirements each tool needs to meet to qualify and participate. The results in our paper are also available on the Test-Comp 21 website. Finally, instructions for building *FuSeBMC* from the source code are given in the file README.md in our GitHub repository, including the description of all dependencies.

A.3   Tool Setup

FuSeBMC is available to download from the link.[3] To generate test cases for a C program a command of the following form is run:

```
fusebmc.py [-a {32, 64}] [-p PROPERTY_FILE]
           [-s {kinduction,falsi,incr,fixed}] [<file>.c]
```

where -a sets the architecture (either 32- or 64-bit), -p sets the property file path, -s sets the strategy (one of kinduction, falsi, incr, or fixed) and <file>.c is the C program to be checked. *FuSeBMC* produces the test cases in the XML format.

---

[3] https://doi.org/10.5281/zenodo.4710599.

References

1. Rodriguez, M., Piattini, M., Ebert, C.: Software verification and validation technologies and tools. IEEE Softw. **36**(2), 13–24 (2019)
2. Airbus issues software bug alert after fatal plane crash. The Guardian, May 2015. https://tinyurl.com/xw67wtd9. Accessed Mar 2021
3. Liu, B., Shi, L., Cai, Z., Li, M.: Software vulnerability discovery techniques: a survey. In: 2012 Fourth International Conference on Multimedia Information Networking and Security, pp. 152–156. IEEE (2012)
4. Clarke, E.M., Emerson, E.A.: Design and synthesis of synchronization skeletons using branching time temporal logic. In: Grumberg, O., Veith, H. (eds.) 25 Years of Model Checking, pp. 196–215 (2008)
5. Godefroid, P.: Fuzzing: hack, art, and science. Commun. ACM **63**(2), 70–76 (2020)
6. Clarke, E.M., Klieber, W., Nováček, M., Zuliani, P.: Model checking and the state explosion problem. In: Meyer, B., Nordio, M. (eds.) LASER 2011. LNCS, vol. 7682, pp. 1–30. Springer, Heidelberg (2012). https://doi.org/10.1007/978-3-642-35746-6_1
7. Shameng, W., Feng Chao, E.A.: Testing network protocol binary software with selective symbolic execution. In: CIS, pp. 318–322. IEEE (2016)
8. Beyer, D.: 3rd competition on software testing (test-comp 2021) (2021)
9. Miller, B.P., et al.: Fuzz revisited: a re-examination of the reliability of UNIX utilities and services. Technical report, UW-Madison (1995)
10. King, J.C.: Symbolic execution and program testing. Commun. ACM **19**(7), 385–394 (1976)
11. Faria, J.: Inspections, revisions and other techniques of software static analysis. Software Testing and Quality, Lecture, vol. 9 (2008)
12. Qin, S., Kim, H.S.: LIFT: a low-overhead practical information flow tracking system for detecting security attacks. In: MICRO 2006, pp. 135–148. IEEE (2006)
13. Ognawala, S., Kilger, F., Pretschner, A.: Compositional fuzzing aided by targeted symbolic execution. arXiv preprint arXiv:1903.02981 (2019)
14. Basak Chowdhury, A., Medicherla, R.K., Venkatesh, R.: VeriFuzz: program aware fuzzing. In: Beyer, D., Huisman, M., Kordon, F., Steffen, B. (eds.) TACAS 2019. LNCS, vol. 11429, pp. 244–249. Springer, Cham (2019). https://doi.org/10.1007/978-3-030-17502-3_22
15. Le, H.M.: LLVM-based hybrid fuzzing with LibKluzzer (competition contribution). In: FASE, pp. 535–539 (2020)
16. Biere, A.: Bounded model checking. In: Biere, A., Heule, M., van Maaren, H., Walsh, T. (eds.) Handbook of Satisfiability. Frontiers in Artificial Intelligence and Applications, vol. 185, pp. 457–481. IOS Press (2009)
17. Cordeiro, L.C., Fischer, B., Marques-Silva, J.: SMT-based bounded model checking for embedded ANSI-C software. IEEE Trans. Software Eng. **38**(4), 957–974 (2012)
18. Beyer, D.: Second competition on software testing: Test-Comp 2020. In: Wehrheim, H., Cabot, J. (eds.) Fundamental Approaches to Software Engineering. FASE 2020. LNCS, vol. 12076, pp. 505–519. Springer, Cham (2020). https://doi.org/10.1007/978-3-030-45234-6_25
19. Cadar, C., Dunbar, D., Engler, D.R.: KLEE: unassisted and automatic generation of high-coverage tests for complex systems programs. In: OSDI, vol. 8, pp. 209–224 (2008)

20. Beyer, D., Keremoglu, M.E.: CPACHECKER: a tool for configurable software verification. In: Gopalakrishnan, G., Qadeer, S. (eds.) CAV 2011. LNCS, vol. 6806, pp. 184–190. Springer, Heidelberg (2011). https://doi.org/10.1007/978-3-642-22110-1_16

21. Alshmrany, K.M., Menezes, R.S., Gadelha, M.R., Cordeiro, L.C.: FuSeBMC: a white-box fuzzer for finding security vulnerabilities in c programs. In: 24th International Conference on Fundamental Approaches to Software Engineering (FASE), vol. 12649, pp. 363–367 (2020)

22. Munea, T.L., Lim, H., Shon, T.: Network protocol fuzz testing for information systems and applications: a survey and taxonomy. Multimedia Tools Appl. **75**(22), 14745–14757 (2016)

23. Wang, J., Guo, T., Zhang, P., Xiao, Q.: A model-based behavioral fuzzing approach for network service. In: 2013 Third International Conference on IMCCC, pp. 1129–1134. IEEE (2013)

24. Baldoni, R., Coppa, E., D'elia, D.C., Demetrescu, C., Finocchi, I.: A survey of symbolic execution techniques. ACM Comput. Surv. **51**, 1–39 (2018)

25. Chipounov, V., Georgescu, V., Zamfir, C., Candea, G.: Selective symbolic execution. In: Proceedings of the 5th Workshop on HotDep (2009)

26. Black, P.E., Bojanova, I.: Defeating buffer overflow: a trivial but dangerous bug. IT Prof. **18**(6), 58–61 (2016)

27. Zhang, S., Zhu, J., Liu, A., Wang, W., Guo, C., Xu, J.: A novel memory leak classification for evaluating the applicability of static analysis tools. In: 2018 IEEE International Conference on Progress in Informatics and Computing (PIC), pp. 351–356. IEEE (2018)

28. Jimenez, W., Mammar, A., Cavalli, A.: Software vulnerabilities, prevention and detection methods: a review. In: Security in Model-Driven Architecture, vol. 215995, p. 215995 (2009)

29. Boudjema, E.H., Faure, C., Sassolas, M., Mokdad, L.: Detection of security vulnerabilities in C language applications. Secur. Priv. **1**(1), e8 (2018)

30. US-CERT: Understanding denial-of-service attacks | CISA (2009)

31. Cisco: Cisco IOS XE software cisco discovery protocol memory leak vulnerability (2018)

32. Clang documentation (2015). http://clang.llvm.org/docs/index.html. Accessed Aug 2019

33. Rocha, H.O., Barreto, R.S., Cordeiro, L.C.: Hunting memory bugs in C programs with Map2Check. In: Chechik, M., Raskin, J.-F. (eds.) TACAS 2016. LNCS, vol. 9636, pp. 934–937. Springer, Heidelberg (2016). https://doi.org/10.1007/978-3-662-49674-9_64

34. Rocha, H., Menezes, R., Cordeiro, L.C., Barreto, R.: Map2Check: using symbolic execution and fuzzing. In: Biere, A., Parker, D. (eds.) Tools and Algorithms for the Construction and Analysis of Systems. TACAS 2020. LNCS, vol. 12079, pp. 403–407. Springer, Cham (2020). https://doi.org/10.1007/978-3-030-45237-7_29

35. Gadelha, M.R., Monteiro, F., Cordeiro, L., Nicole, D.: ESBMC v6.0: verifying C programs using k-induction and invariant inference. In: Beyer, D., Huisman, M., Kordon, F., Steffen, B. (eds.) TACAS 2019. LNCS, vol. 11429, pp. 209–213. Springer, Cham (2019). https://doi.org/10.1007/978-3-030-17502-3_15

36. Gadelha, M.R., Monteiro, F.R., Morse, J., Cordeiro, L.C., Fischer, B., Nicole, D.A.: ESBMC 5.0: an industrial-strength C model checker. In: Proceedings of the 33rd ACM/IEEE International Conference on Automated Software Engineering, pp. 888–891 (2018)

37. Beyer, D., Lemberger, T.: TestCov: robust test-suite execution and coverage measurement. In: 2019 34th IEEE/ACM International Conference on Automated Software Engineering (ASE), pp. 1074–1077. IEEE (2019)
38. Lopes, B.C., Auler, R.: Getting started with LLVM core libraries. Packt Publishing Ltd. (2014)
39. Beyer, D.: Status report on software testing: Test-Comp 2021. In: Guerra, E., Stoelinga, M. (eds.) Fundamental Approaches to Software Engineering FASE 2021. LNCS, vol. 12649, pp. 341–357. Springer, Cham (2021). https://doi.org/10.1007/978-3-030-71500-7_17
40. Beyer, D.: Software verification: 10th comparative evaluation (SV-COMP 2021). In: Groote, J.F., Larsen, K.G. (eds.) Tools and Algorithms for the Construction and Analysis of Systems. TACAS 2021. LNCS, vol. 12652, pp. 401–422. Springer, Cham (2021). https://doi.org/10.1007/978-3-030-72013-1_24
41. Chalupa, M., Novák, J., Strejček, J.: SYMBIOTIC 8: parallel and targeted test generation. FASE 2021. LNCS, vol. 12649, pp. 368–372. Springer, Cham (2021). https://doi.org/10.1007/978-3-030-71500-7_20
42. Beyer, D., Wendler, P.: CPU energy meter: a tool for energy-aware algorithms engineering. TACAS 2020. LNCS, vol. 12079, pp. 126–133. Springer, Cham (2020). https://doi.org/10.1007/978-3-030-45237-7_8
43. Barton, J.H., Czeck, E.W., Segall, Z.Z., Siewiorek, D.P.: Fault injection experiments using fiat. IEEE Trans. Comput. **39**(4), 575–582 (1990)
44. Böhme, M., Pham, V.-T., Nguyen, M.-D., Roychoudhury, A.: Directed greybox fuzzing. In: Proceedings of the 2017 ACM SIGSAC Conference on Computer and Communications Security, pp. 2329–2344 (2017)
45. American fuzzy lop (2021). https://lcamtuf.coredump.cx/afl/
46. Serebryany, K.: libFuzzer-a library for coverage-guided fuzz testing. LLVM project (2015)
47. Gorbunov, S., Rosenbloom, A.: AutoFuzz: automated network protocol fuzzing framework. IJCSNS **10**(8), 239 (2010)
48. Eddington, M.: Peach fuzzing platform. Peach Fuzzer, vol. 34 (2011)
49. Jaffar, J., Maghareh, R., Godboley, S., Ha, X.-L.: TracerX: dynamic symbolic execution with interpolation (competition contribution). In: FASE, pp. 530–534 (2020)
50. Song, J., Cadar, C., Pietzuch, P.: SymbexNet: testing network protocol implementations with symbolic execution and rule-based specifications. In: IEEE TSE, vol. 40, no. 7, pp. 695–709 (2014)
51. Sasnauskas, R., Kaiser, P., Jukić, R.L., Wehrle, K.: Integration testing of protocol implementations using symbolic distributed execution. In: ICNP, pp. 1–6. IEEE (2012)
52. Le, H.M.: LLVM-based hybrid fuzzing with LibKluzzer (competition contribution). In: Wehrheim, H., Cabot, J. (eds.) Fundamental Approaches to Software Engineering. FASE 2020. LNCS, vol. 12076, pp. 535–539. Springer, Cham (2020). https://doi.org/10.1007/978-3-030-45234-6_29
53. Stephens, N., et al.: Driller: augmenting fuzzing through selective symbolic execution. In: NDSS, pp. 1–16 (2016)
54. Pak, B.S.: Hybrid fuzz testing: discovering software bugs via fuzzing and symbolic execution. School of Computer Science Carnegie Mellon University (2012)
55. Noller, Y., Kersten, R., Păsăreanu, C.S.: Badger: complexity analysis with fuzzing and symbolic execution. In: Proceedings of the 27th ACM SIGSOFT International Symposium on Software Testing and Analysis, pp. 322–332 (2018)

56. Păsăreanu, C.S., Rungta, N.: Symbolic pathfinder: symbolic execution of Java byte-code. In: Proceedings of the IEEE/ACM International Conference on Automated Software Engineering, pp. 179–180 (2010)
57. Ognawala, S., Hutzelmann, T., Psallida, E., Pretschner, A.: Improving function coverage with munch: a hybrid fuzzing and directed symbolic execution approach. In: Proceedings of the 33rd Annual ACM Symposium on Applied Computing, pp. 1475–1482 (2018)
58. Godefroid, P., Levin, M.Y., Molnar, D.: SAGE: whitebox fuzzing for security testing. Queue **10**(1), 20–27 (2012)
59. Wang, M., et al.: SAFL: increasing and accelerating testing coverage with symbolic execution and guided fuzzing. In: Proceedings of the 40th International Conference on Software Engineering: Companion Proceedings, pp. 61–64 (2018)
60. He, J., Balunović, M., Ambroladze, N., Tsankov, P., Vechev, M.: Learning to fuzz from symbolic execution with application to smart contracts. In: Proceedings of the 2019 ACM SIGSAC Conference on Computer and Communications Security, pp. 531–548 (2019)
61. Cordeiro, L.C.: SMT-based bounded model checking for multi-threaded software in embedded systems. In: International Conference on Software Engineering, pp. 373–376. ACM (2010)
62. Pereira, P.A., et al.: Verifying CUDA programs using SMT-based context-bounded model checking. In: Ossowski, S. (ed.) Annual ACM Symposium on Applied Computing, pp. 1648–1653. ACM (2016)

Author Index

Printed in the United States
by Baker & Taylor Publisher Services